A River of Stories

By

The Tulsa Nightwriters

Table of Contents

Part 1. Historicals and Westerns

Part 2. Poetry and Essays

Part 3. Modern Fiction

Historicals and Westerns

"Sand Plum Summer"

by

Carla Stewart

Lumbering along in the heat, Clyde Jenkins almost missed the haggard sign that hung off-kilter on a fence post. He slowed the roadster, dust boiling up behind him as he took in the tired, faded lettering. Tucker County. More desolate than he'd imagined, the landscape lay raw and ravaged by wind and dirt. No wonder hordes before him had beaten a path to a better life out west. California. The Promised Land.

Heat shimmers rose, bending the landscape into earthen and slate layers, blurring the horizon. Off to his left, Clyde caught a flash in the undergrowth. A jackrabbit, no doubt. How anything could survive in this shriveled corner of the world staggered him. How, indeed?

Another flicker—a blur of pink. He swiped a handkerchief across his forehead and scanned the dried up plain. God Almighty had granted no mercy here.

His eyes wandered, mindful that he'd arrived at his destination. He patted the map atop a newspaper on the seat beside him. Now, if only. . .

A young girl with a bucket dangling from her arm popped from the brambles alongside the road. Her pink blouse seemed a mirage, vivid in the still settling dust he'd stirred up. Round, brown eyes peered at him, curious and inquisitive, no hint of wariness.

"Say, miss, I'm looking for a place called Paris, Oklahoma. Is this the right road?"

She scrambled up a shallow embankment, waving away the dust with one hand, clinging to the bucket with the other.

"Yes, sir. You's about there. Just a mile over yonder." She tilted her head to the west, then squinted her eyes and looked him square in the face.

"Say, Mister, you ever eaten a sand plum?" She held out a handful of the pale red nuggets.

"Guess I haven't. A bit puny, aren't they?" He reached his hand out to take one, thought better of it, and instead, pulled on the door handle. The solid ground felt good to his legs as he stepped into the heat.

"Umm-huh. Takes near a gallon of 'em to get two good pies. But we just boil 'em up and Maw makes the best plum butter you ever laid on a piece a bread."

"Sounds fine, miss, but I better not keep you from your work. I'll just stretch and get on my way."

"What's yer hurry? Come set a spell and have some."

"Thanks. Maybe for just a minute." They tottered down the sand of the creek bank, the sun high overhead. A mere sliver of shade was all the scraggly bushes had to offer.

"Tell me about yourself." Clyde eyed the sun-browned legs and golden pigtails of the small, forthright girl. Not more than ten or twelve, he guessed. Enchanting little thing.

"You ain't one of them paper reporters, are ya?" Cocking her head, she gazed up at him.

"No."

"Good. They's been quite a few of 'em showed up here. Everbody got all worked up at first, being's how they wanted to get our stories about surviving the dirt storms. After a while, though, we was plumb wore out talking about it. And nobody ever sent no papers back telling the stuff we said."

"I guess they did write those stories. I read quite a few of them out in California."

"That where yer from, Mister?"

"Not originally. Went out a couple of years back."

"Then how come you're asking about Paris?"

"You're sure full of questions, aren't you, Missy?" He had a few questions of his own. Being so close to what he'd come after, Clyde felt determination coursing through his veins.

"I figure if I want to know something, being nosy's the best way."

"Guess you're right about that. You have a name?" He popped a sand plum into his mouth.

"Liberty Barlow."

Clyde sucked in the sour juice of the fruit and nearly choked. Barlow. Yes, he was close. He wiped his lips with the back of his hand and peered at the small girl. My God, this couldn't be one of them. No, he'd remember, even after three years. But she might be the one to help him.

"I's born on the Fourth of July, on the one hundred and fiftieth birthday of our country. Maw wanted to call me Jessie, after my paw, but Paw wouldn't have none of it. Said if I's born on such a commemorating day, I oughta have a fitting name. So, you can call me Liberty. What's your name?"

"Clyde Jenkins."

"What'd them papers say about us, Mr. Jenkins?"

The hairs on the back of his neck snapped to attention. "They told how you braved the drought and the dust, compared you to the pioneers. Quite a lot of stories, really. Why don't you tell me yours?" A thread of hope shot through him. Until that moment, he hadn't dared to imagine he'd actually find out the fate of his sister and her three young children. Two weeks before Easter in '35, she'd packed up and left Missouri to head west. So many had gone looking for a dream. He knew, for her, survival was the dream. Now, standing here beside this Barlow child, he felt the raw truth so close he could taste it.

Liberty straightened. "I been living right here on the edge of Minnow Creek my whole life. Paris is a mile down the road, which I already told ya. If the wind is outta the south, you can spit plumb into Kansas." She snatched a stick lying in the sand and drew lines and circles in the earth below. "Things is better now the drought's letting up. We'd a gone to California, like you Mister, if it'd hung on much longer. Daddy had to shoot Miz Millicent, our Guernsey, 'cuz there weren't a speck of grass for her to eat."

She tossed the stick into the lazy current of water. "This creek used to be drier than a mouthful o' soda crackers, but some o' the old-timers talked about pulling catfish outta there as long as your arm in the homesteading days."

Tucker County. It had been the object of his obsession since he'd read the two-column article about three children left orphaned following the worst dirt storm in recorded history. Black Sunday, the papers called it. Unable to shake the gnawing in his belly, he'd set out. His need to lay it at rest propelled him to find the truth. Now, some small part of him hesitated.

Liberty plopped beside him. "What I remember most was them awful clouds boiling up outta nowhere. Me and Maw would grab an armful a rags and soak 'em up real good and put 'em around the windows to stop the dirt. Didn't help much. About the time we'd get the mess cleaned up, here'd come another storm. Maw would shake out my covers 'fore she tucked me in and tell me stories about blue skies and birds singing. I just couldn't imagine." She gave him a sideward glance. "Me, I had my own dreams, but not about skies and birds. Know what I'd dream about, Mister?"

"Couldn't guess."

Liberty wrinkled her turned-up nose. "Ever since I can remember I wanted a baby brother. So every night I prayed real hard. Preacher Bohannon said, 'Delight thyself also in the Lord; and He shall give thee the desires of thine heart.' I did my chores and said my prayers every day, and lo and behold, I got the desire of my heart."

"Your momma had a baby?"

"Nope. One Sunday morning, Maw was smiling and humming 'Amazing Grace' when she got me out of bed. She hurried me outside to look at the pertiest blue sky you ever saw. She just kept going on about our prayers being answered. I's afraid to ask about the baby brother, so I just figured she meant her dream of the blue skies. And ya know, right then, three robins came up to our porch and sang a song for us. Maw had tears running down her cheeks. We stood there so long, we had to hurry like a house afire to make it to the church before the 'Doxology.'"

Liberty rose to her feet and skipped along the sand to the water's edge. Putting in the toes of one bare foot, then the other, she gave a kick and waded until the water covered her ankles. Sunlight lit the strands of hair that escaped her braids. "Say, Mister, you got any kids?"

"No, Liberty, not of my own."

When she swooped up an armful of water, rays of purple and crimson glinted off the spray. She laughed and returned to the shade, her feet orange from the clinging sand.

"I got something to show ya." Liberty motioned with her arm and her head.

Clyde followed, ducking under the sticky tamarack branches. Her darting figure reminded him of his childhood, playing along the Missouri riverbanks with his sister Lorna Beth. Carefree, happy years before she married Finster Poole. A familiar constriction squeezed his chest. He stopped to catch his breath and spat in the sand when bile rose in his throat. Bile brought forth by the memory of Finster Poole. No wonder Lorna Beth headed west first chance she got. Nine years of hell with a moon shiner who spent every ill-gotten dime he made on cock fights, leaving Lorna Beth to provide however she could for herself and their three innocent children.

Liberty stopped and pointed at a wooden hut before them. The solitary window had boards nailed haphazardly across it, while the door, no more than four feet high, clung to the shanty on one hinge.

"This is where we found 'em."

"Found what? Who?" Clyde's mouth went dry.

"Why, Maggie, Ruthie, and the baby. Weren't ya listening? It was two days after the robins sang. I told ya, we was at church, and afterwards, we had a basket lunch. All us kids played while the grown-ups sat around talking about if it rains. There mighta been one or two little white puffs in the sky.

"Gertie just called out, 'Red Rover, Red Rover, let Liberty come over,' when the sky turned all funny looking. A blast of cold air near sucked out my lungs, and it blew my dress up around my ears. Mean, black clouds boiled up from the edges of the earth. I thought it was the devil. Paw grabbed me under his arm and threw me in the truck. The ladies' hats was flying through the air, and smack, one o' Sheriff Smith's Rhode Island Reds slammed into our windshield. Feathers and chicken poop everywhere."

Liberty's eyes flashed and her breath came in little quick spurts as she continued.

"It happened so fast, people got scattered ever which way. Next day, they sent search parties looking for stragglers. The second day, Paw found 'em hunched in the corner yonder. When he brung 'em to the house, they looked like tar babies, they's so black from the dirt blown around 'em. Maw and me cleaned 'em up real good in the washtub. And that's how I got me two sisters and a baby brother." She tilted her chin and smiled.

Clyde thought an angel could not be more beautiful.

Liberty yanked the door free from the weeds. Squinting his eyes, Clyde looked over her shoulder into the dark shed. A drift of powdery silt inclined toward the far wall. A rat scurried into a hole leaving a snake-like furrow with its tail across the slope.

Heaviness rested on Clyde's shoulders. He knew far more than he'd ever dreamed he'd find out. He grappled with the weight of it. What he'd do now, he wasn't sure. The children were his nieces and nephew, he knew for certain. Maggie, Ruthie, and Chester, the baby named after his own father, Chester Jenkins.

"Liberty, that's quite an experience for a young girl, but I've kept you too long. You need to be getting home or your folks will be worried." Clyde needed to get on, too. Agony gnawed his gut. He wished he hadn't written his kin in Missouri about the newspaper article. Especially Finster Poole.

"It's okay. Maw and Paw took the little 'uns to town. But I best be getting my plums washed up for Maw to cook later on. Nice talking to ya." She scooped up the bucket and scrambled off, toward a farmhouse where she disappeared behind a screen door. A fresh coat of paint gleamed on the wooden shingles of the Barlow home.

Clyde stood a moment and took it all in before climbing into the driver's seat.

~

"Sheriff Smith, here. And who might you be?"

"Clyde Jenkins. Los Angeles. I'm doing a follow-up report on a story we ran awhile back. Do you remember . . ." He said a prayer of thanks for Liberty giving him the reporter angle. For now, it seemed the best way to conclude the business that brought him to Paris.

The sheriff remained seated and leaned forward on his elbows. "Tragic happening, finding those kids. Story goes their mother had headed west with another family, taking the kids with her. God only knows why a woman would run off and leave her husband, but that's the setup we got. Best as we could ever figure out, she separated herself from the others up in Kansas and holed up in the shack down on Minnow Creek.

No reports from people in town about seeing them; the only evidence comes from the oldest girl musta been about seven or eight at the time it happened. Told the Barlows her mother left to find something to eat Sunday morning. Course you know what happened in the afternoon. Nobody caught in that tempest from hell could have survived."

The Sheriff leaned back and sucked on a piece of wheat straw.

"Did they ever find the mother?" Clyde willed himself to keep breathing.

"Near as we can tell, they found her remains over on the Simmons place when he worked up a patch of ground. Spookiest thing I ever saw parts of her dress hanging on the bones. We showed the girl the ragged piece, and she verified her mother had a dress similar. Any particular slant you're taking?"

An ache rested in the hollow spot in Clyde's chest. He swallowed hard. "Just a follow up. We wanted to get a report on the kids. Sort of a human-interest thing. Did the kids end up all right?"

"Fine as frog hair. They're out at the Barlow's. They took in all three of them to raise with their little girl. Hard working and God fearing, that's Jess Barlow. Made his missus happy, too. Yes, sir. Those kids are all right."

"Thanks, Sheriff. I'll be giving you the credit for passing on this information. Good day."

Clyde didn't hesitate when he stepped into his roadster. He filled it with gas and headed west. One thing for certain, he wouldn't be going to Missouri. He'd wire Finster Poole from Albuquerque or Phoenix, far away from these parts, and give him the regretful news he'd found out nothing about his missing wife and children. Somehow, he didn't think Finster would spend any time grieving.

~

Liberty had just finished washing the plums when Maw and Paw came in. Mrs. Barlow started the water boiling for the jam, and Liberty set the table.

After grace, Jess looked at Liberty. "Say, sugar, we met a car going into town when we were coming home. Nobody we knew. You didn't see anyone passing while you were out picking today, did you?"

Liberty took a big gulp of milk and shook her head so the pigtails slapped the sides of her face.

"Good. I don't like you kids talking to strangers, you know."

"Yes, Paw. I know you don't. Would you pass the potatoes, please?"

~

In mid-November, a letter arrived and Jess Barlow read it at the supper table.

Dear Mr. and Mrs. Barlow,

I read with interest the account of your taking in three young children left destitute after Black Sunday, 1935.

Enclosed you will find a "Baby Bond" for each of your children. I hope they will be useful sometime in the future.

God bless.

Clyde Jenkins

"If that don't beat all." Jess Barlow thumbed through the certificates. "Why, look here, there's four bonds. How in tarnation did he know there were four Barlow kids?"

Liberty studied the pale pink roses on her plate.

"I'll have some more plum butter, please."

The Family Tree
by
Bill Wetterman

"Papa, hurry up or you'll be late."

"Give me some time." The impatience of the young irritated Miklos Novotny. Dressing for church took meticulous planning and care, especially with his heart aching. He missed his wife, Anna. How does one get used to waking up alone? After thirty-four years of marriage, she wasn't here for him to hold and care for anymore. His gnarled fingers ached as he slowly crammed each button of his thick tweed sweater into its eyehole. He called through the door to his son. "Edward, do you have my bowler?"

"Yes." Edward swore under his breath in Slovak, and Miklos could hear him pacing on the other side of the bedroom door.

He sighed. People handled grief in different ways. He had to remind himself he wasn't the only one who had lost someone dear to him. He wrapped his scarf about his neck and glanced around his bedroom one more time. Anna's hand had painted warmth into this room. She'd stitched a honey colored

[21]

quilt, carefully blending maple leaves and stems in varying shades of green throughout. She'd helped him repaint the walls a peaceful gold.

He'd handcrafted the furniture from maple wood and laid a hardwood floor of a matching maple color, while she wove the brown and gold rugs. Since then, nineteen years had passed. Still the room appeared recently refinished. He took a deep breath as his eyes rested on her portrait.

"Papa!"

"All right."

Miklos opened the bedroom door, tucked his scarf into his coat, and headed with his son and his family to Saint Stephen's Catholic Church.

~

Heavy wet snow covered the landscape on the drive from Florence into Caldwell, Ohio. Winters could be brutal. Miklos was helped up the stairs and through the doors into the small, dimly-lit church by Edward and his daughter-in-law Beatrice. Thirty-two years in the mines had eaten away at his lungs. He stopped several times to catch his breath.

"How are you doing Mick?" a neighbor whispered.

"I'm fine."

As his eyes adjusted to the light, he realized fewer than forty people were in the church, mostly his children and friends from the mines. Heaviness fell on his soul. Anna deserved better. Still he made the sign-of-the-cross, genuflected, and hobbled to his seat on the front row. "You see, Edward, we're here in plenty of time. Your mother's sister Cecilia isn't here yet. Where are Mary and Victoria?"

"They live too far away. No one else is coming." Edward helped his father sit.

"Surely they're just late."

"I've talked to them. Mary and Victoria can't make it in from Cleveland."

"They're our daughters. My God, they should find a way."

Milkos' lower lip quivered and he fought back tears. A man must never cry, he thought. Poor Stephan, his oldest son, still lay in an unmarked grave somewhere in France. Now Anna had joined his spirit in God's house. At least they weren't alone. His daughter, Juliana, and her husband, Karl, sat in the pew directly behind him. Betty, the third of his six children, sat next to her sister, Mary. Now Sister Mary Novotny, she looked as beautiful as the statute of Saint Teresa positioned at the left side of the altar. Anna would have been pleased.

"All rise."

Father Karhnak entered behind two altar boys who carried the Bible and the water and wine vials. *"In nomine Patris et filli et Spiritus Sancti . . ."*

Miklos grabbed his kerchief and quickly dabbed his eyes. No one else was coming? His heart ached. In Europe, family came to share in the grieving.

~

The snow fell harder as a caravan of six cars followed the hearse to the family burial site on the east side of the Novotny property. Only relatives and the clergy were allowed here. The other twenty-five guests waited back at the church eating a wholesome lunch. Miklos pulled his long wool coat tight and limped up the slope to the gravesite with his daughters on each arm. Edward and Beatrice assisted Father Karhnak by issuing instructions and directing family to the make-shift tent by the grave.

The headstone read: Anna Jedlicka Novotny, born April 5, 1874 in *Spaski Stara Ves*, Austria – Died January 12, 1929 in Florence, Ohio, USA. On the stone next to Anna's was engraved: Miklos Edward Novotny, born October 14, 1859 in Bratislava, Austria – Died . . . Both his mother and Anna were buried here along with his brother August.

I will come to you soon my love.

"Are you able to stand?" Juliana asked, her dark gypsy-like eyes sparkling like her mother's used to.

"I'm fine. I will not sit like a cripple and dishonor your mother. God rest her soul." His daughter hugged him and he whispered, "Tonight, at the house, come please. I need time alone with you, Betty, and Edward."

"I'll have to arm-wrestle Eddie, but he'll be there."

Miklos nodded and made the sign of the cross "Rest in peace, *boh s vami.*"

"God is with her, Papa."

When Father Karhnak finished his comments, Anna's body was lowered into the grave. Miklos planted his feet and didn't move until the earth covered the top of the casket. As his daughters helped him back down the hill, four of his grandchildren ran up asking questions about their Baba Anna. "How old was she?" "What did she die from?" "Will you have to live by yourself?"

He rested against Edward's Model A Roadster and the crisp clean air smelled like pine-scented ice cones. "Baba caught pneumonia little ones. She was only fifty-four." Anna's glowing face came to his mind and brightened his spirits. "But I will not be alone. God and Baba's memory are always my companions."

"Get in the car. You'll be the next with pneumonia if you don't take care of yourself." Edward, with Beatrice in tow, shooed Juliana's kids back to their car and set his two boys in the back seat. "What's this meeting tonight about? I'd think you'd be too tired to stay up and talk."

"It's about your inheritance."

With that Edward straightened up, and Beatrice aggressively tugged his arm. "What time do you want me there?"

"When our guests are gone and the children are fed and in bed, come to the house."

"Thanks for letting us stay in the Bezub's old place."

"No thanks needed. No one lives in any of the houses on the hill, but me. You can visit anytime and stay in any house you choose. I keep them spotless."

Edward grunted, and Miklos knew a visit from his son in the future was unlikely. He chuckled softly as the snow fell lightly through the trees. Until tonight then, he thought. Tonight he'd learn how well he and Anna had raised their children.

~

The hall grandfather clock struck eight in the evening followed by the chime of his pocket watch a few moments later. Miklos grunted, musing that he could never keep the chimes in unison. He turned on his vaporizer and rubbed mentholated-jelly on his chest. The mines had stolen his youth and black lung had robbed him of energy. His conversation with his children would require strength and extreme patience.

Betty and Juliana arrived first covered with snow and red-faced. "The old Jedlicka house is farther from here than it was when I was eight," Betty said. "Or maybe this young nun hasn't been exercising."

"I can't walk that far anymore." Miklos took their coats and hung them by the door. "I use Belle and the cart."

"Oh Belle, I'd forgotten about the mule."

"Sit down," he said, and waved his hand toward the couch. He opened the fireplace vent a little to allow for more

[27]

heat. Then he walked over to a small cedar chest, unlatched it, and reached inside. He carefully pulled out an object wrapped in pure white linen and set it on the coffee table in the center of the living room.

The sound of heavy boots on the steps startled Juliana. Two loud bangs on the door and it swung open. Edward Novotny stepped inside. "If a door is unlocked, I assume I'm invited in."

"Here you are correct." Miklos grinned. "Try that at one of the neighbors, and you'll have a seat full of buckshot to deal with."

Edward tossed his coat on the bench near the door instead of hanging it up. He rushed into the living room and plopped down on Baba's French lounger. He focused his steel blue eyes on Miklos. "So let's talk."

Miklos noticed the coat and wondered if Edward planned to stay long. "Tea?"

A strong "No Thank You" erupted from each of his children.

"Are you all in a hurry?"

"I'm not," Juliana said. "Karl's a capable sitter."

Edward's face appeared as though it would crack at the jaws, and he squirmed uncomfortably. What Miklos had to say wouldn't make him any happier.

"There is little I have in the way of money." Miklos looked down at his shoes. "Maybe I can get along a few more years without selling the houses and the land."

His son's face reddened. "And whose fault is that?"

"I don't understand."

"My God, Eddie," Betty whispered, one hand over her mouth. "Leave it alone. Can't you see he's grieving?"

"No. Tonight we put everything out on the table."

"I agree," Miklos said. "What's bothering you?"

"Mama went without the nice things in life." His son's face trembled. "She raised six kids, cooked, cleaned, and never complained. And for what—these rundown houses on this hill?"

"You have no interest in living in them?"

"None whatsoever."

Heavyhearted, Miklos pulled a pipe out of his sweater pocket and bounced the bowl on his hand. "Every decision Mama and I made we made together. We sacrificed for our families in Europe and for you children."

"Now that your family's here, they don't give a shit about us."

"Eddie, stop." Juliana grabbed Edward's sleeve. "They did what they thought was best. Except for Mary, we're all doing all right. It her own fault she's become who she is."

Miklos' jaw tightened. "Always our families hoped for someone to have the good fortune to come to America. God appointed me. My coming was His gift. My relatives helped me travel here from Europe. And I helped as many as I could make it here to America as well. So don't judge your mother or me."

Edward pushed back firmly against the sofa cushions and crossed his legs. He shook his finger. "When was the last time Aunt Cecilia or Aunt Katrina visited you? Your own brother came here from Europe, stayed a year in Ohio, and left for California. He never visited again before he died."

"Mama talked to her sisters by phone at least once a week. It's hard when you live ninety miles away. We never visited them either. Not everyone owns a Model A like yours." He packed his pipe and lit it. The pungent smell of hickory tobacco filled the air. "Yes, I brought my brother,

August, and my mother here. I brought your mama's brother and four sisters here. And yes, it cost money."

"You left us kids here for weeks at a time." Edward shook his head. "While you took off and met every one of those ungrateful toads at the port in New York, we worked and paid the bills. How much did it cost us over the years?"

"Hard work never hurt anyone." Miklos felt his face flush, pounded the coffee table, and pointed at Edward. "They're not ungrateful toads. They're family. It was worth it to give a good life to them and their children. Besides I used vacation time."

Juliana gasped. Betty pursed her lips. Miklos coughed and spit-up phlegm into an old handkerchief.

"You shouldn't be smoking." Betty fingered the rosary beads that were hooked on the belt at the side of her habit. "With all the coal dust in your lungs, the smoke could kill you."

He disregarded her comment with a wave of his hand and swallowed his temper. "Enough said on the topic of our family. I see you perceive them differently. But I have something to show you." Miklos leaned forward and picked up the object he'd place on the table earlier. He carefully removed the white linen covering to reveal a black leather-engraved Bible. His hands moved over the surface as if it were a holy relic. "This isn't just a Bible. It's a historical record."

"Mama told me you kept the family genealogy." Juliana's eyes ignited with joy, and she put her hand atop her father's. "So it's in this Bible?"

"Yes. Two older Bibles fell apart from age. After my brother August died, the Bible was mailed to me."

Miklos opened the top cover. He smiled. The Bible had several lined pages reserved for family records. At the top of the first page was handwritten, Stanislaus Popovich Novotny, *rok nàsho Pàna,* 1493. Under that notation, neatly printed, was the Novotny family tree. Notations continued right up until this day on every yellowed space the Bible provided.

"The first two hundred years of records were recorded from memory. Afterward the records were recorded as they occurred. Now it's coming close to the end of my time, and I must pass the Bible along."

"Amazing," Juliana said. "It even tells their occupations."

"What about the houses and the land?" Edward asked. "If you sell them, how will the money be divided?"

Miklos cracked his knuckles and stared at his son. "Fairly."

Edward got up and grabbed his coat. "Let Juliana have the Bible. If there's nothing more, I'm going."

"One more thing." Miklos pulled the cedar chest over next to him and reached inside. "I carved these for your sons."

Out of the chest came a chessboard and a bag holding two sets of chess men. One set was finished in maple and the other in a deep mahogany stain. Each square of the board was inset and carefully fit. The board had been rubbed so finely it shone brightly in the light of the room. Even if their father was a nincompoop, Miklos could not deny his grandsons. He handed the chess game to Edward.

Edward's countenance warmed. "Thank you, Papa. These are marvelous."

Miklos edged to his feet and hugged his son. Edward stiffened slightly, turned, and left without another word.

"Betty, is that your wish too?"

"That Juliana takes the Bible?"

"Yes." He eased back into his chair.

"Of course it is. My life is full." She squeezed her sister's hand while giving her father an affectionate nod. "I don't need an inheritance, and I'll have no descendants to pass the Bible to. Juliana should have it."

"Then that's settled." He pointed to the small cedar chest. "Tomorrow, before you go Juliana, you and Karl come and take this chest and what's in it. I've crafted gifts for all my grandchildren. Each gift is unique to the child. There's one for Victoria's daughter in Cleveland. See that she gets it when she's eight."

"I'd be delighted. But why don't you give it to her then?"

"If I'm around, I'm sure you'll remind me."

Juliana sighed. "I'm sorry about Eddie. Someday he'll understand what family means. But he has a point. It was hard for us to see you spend your time and money on our relatives."

The gentle sting in her words cut him. Had he sacrificed only to anger his own children?

The thought still bothered him that so few relatives showed up at Anna's funeral. If he'd traveled as far as New York multiple times for his family, how could a trip from Newcomerstown or Cleveland keep Anna's two daughters or her sister from coming?

"Would you ever want to live in these homes?" he asked Juliana.

A condescending head tilt told him the answer before she spoke. "They hold no good memories for me. Not like they do for you. Besides, Karl is a good provider."

"So be it, then. I'll take on the burden of disposing of them."

~

By nine-thirty that evening, the house again stood empty of family. Miklos straightened and cleaned. The unused tea cups were stowed away. The chest was closed and set by the door for Juliana to take the next morning. Miklos cleaned his pipe as he sat and rocked by the warmth of the hearth. He laid aside the pipe cleaners for a moment, picked up the telephone from its black cradle, and listened. He heard the dial tone and no voices speaking, so he was safe to dial. It had only been a year since the phone company eliminated their switchboard. He placed his call to Father Karhnak direct.

"Is your family meeting over, Mick?" Father said after Miklos identified himself.

"Unfortunately so."

"Things went as we expected then?"

"Yes, Father John, exactly as we expected." Miklos pulled out a pad and pencil. "What does the Diocese propose?"

"Archbishop Higgins has drafted a document offering fifty thousand dollars for the land, houses, and cemetery. The conditions are as follows: your family plot will not be disturbed. The Diocese will tear down the houses. We'll create a Catholic cemetery and build the necessary offices on the land."

"Our deal, Father, is it still good?"

"Absolutely. Since your home is close to the road and well away from the cemetery grounds, you can stay there rent free for the rest of your life."

Miklos chuckled. "Then you'll bury me in my plot."

"I'll call you when the document arrives."

~

The wind had picked up by midnight. It howled around the house, but inside it was warm. "Did we do the right thing my love?" he said aloud.

He and Anna knew what life was like in the old country before they left. Their children and grandchildren would never understand. In one sense he thanked God. But in another sense he felt his children were cheated. They never experienced the close devotion of family, one where you needn't be face-to-face to feel their love.

Miklos closed his eyes and said his evening prayers. Tomorrow he would finalize his Last Will and Testament. He would appoint Juliana as executor and put five thousand dollars in each of his grandchildren's names to be used for their education. If America was the land of dreams, a private school education was the ticket to fulfill them. Juliana would have ten thousand dollars remaining, and if no other grandchildren came along, she would divide the remaining funds among her brothers and sisters.

Other than money for food and utilities, he had nothing left. But he needed nothing more, except feed for Belle. A momentary wisp of sadness flowed over him that Victoria and Mary never came from Cleveland. But he'd been the best father he knew how to be. The rest was between them and their God. "Good night, *moja làska*."

Somewhere in his mind he heard Anna answer him with a sweet and reassuring voice, "Good night my love. I'll see you soon."

The Family Tree placed seventh in the Writers' Digest Short Story competition out of 11,700 plus entries.

AGNESE

by

Maggie Villines

Agnese Fermi shuddered as she unlocked the door of Fermi Photography and slipped inside. Desperate to get off the street, away from the stares, she left the 'Closed' sign in place, walked to the studio wall, and lifted a framed photo from its hook. In the backroom, she propped it against a dictionary on her desk. With one hand, she wiped away tears. With the other, her finger jabbed at the face of each man, as she said his name aloud. She pulled the photo's proofs from the files, and with the picture, hid them behind equipment in the darkroom — instinctive preparation for the dark times ahead — anticipating the need to protect her husband, Elia. The year was 1938.

Two years earlier, Chiano Ruber, a member of the Fascist Party's Jewish Coalition, hired Elia Fermi to take the official group photo of the Jews representing Northern Italia's Piedmont region. That day Simona Gallo, from the deli down the street, sat gossiping with Agnese in the studio. As Simona opened the door to leave, Ruber was standing there,

[39]

unmoving, staring at her. She avoided his eyes and squeezed past him. His girth and his garlic breath filled the room. Agnese fought the urge to cover her nose.

So much garlic? At nine in the morning? Fat, old fool.

"Signora, get your husband for me," he said.

Signora? "It's Agnese, Chiano. Elia is out, but should be back in fifteen minutes."

He rested the palms of both hands on the showroom table where she sat, and leaned toward her. "I stopped by last week, Signora Fermi — last week, and your husband was on his way out. I represent the government. You understand?"

Hairs prickled on her arms.

"Elia told me he explained the circumstances. He was so grateful that you understood. It couldn't be avoided. Won't you please sit down? He should be...."

"I have no time," he said, and with his hands, pushed his ponderous bulk away from the table. He turned his gaze to the walls lined with Elia's photography, much of it considered works of art.

"Would you like a coffee?"

"Achhhh, no time, Signora Fermi, no time!"

The door opened and Elia's long legs steered him through the door to greet Ruber. The dickering over the price of a photo session began within seconds of saying hello.

"Elia, if you need me, I'll be in the backroom, throwing up." Neither man heard, or glanced her way. He will give away our grocery money to make that man happy, she thought.

Agnese heard the bell on the door jingle as Ruber left.

"He's gone, *amore mio*," Elia said, as he walked to the back of her chair, and wrapped his arms about her, nestling his mouth close to her ear. "You threw-up," he chuckled. "Could you smell the garlic? Oh *mio*, even in Italia that was too much, too early."

She shrugged out of his arms and turned to him. "Fascism is no kind of liberty, Elia. Nothing good will come of this. The coalition is blind to the danger coming. I don't know how they can be, but they are. Blind, deaf, and bloated with arrogance, not to mention rude."

"One of three Jews in Torino is a Fascist, Agnese."

"But not you, Elia!"

He shoved his hands deep into his pants pockets and shrugged his shoulders. "I am not, but these people are my friends, and they mean me no harm."

"Elia, darling, you are guileless. Fascism is not. Fascism will not allow us to live in peace. Mussolini will not resist Hitler."

~

She pushed away the memory of that day with Ruber, and pulled the morning issue of Journal of Italia from her satchel. "Fascism and the problem of race," pulsed at her from the front page. Bile rose in her throat, as it had at breakfast when she read Mussolini's Manifesto of Racist Scientists for the first time. Il Duce, he calls himself! The Chief! Italia will not survive this. She opened the newspaper and smoothed it with her hand. Looking down the page to the Manifesto's declarations, she reread three of them:

9. Jews do not belong to the Italian race.

6. There exists by now a pure 'Italian race.'

7. It is time that the Italians proclaim themselves frankly racist.

She read it again:

9. Jews do not belong to the Italian race.

The morning sun streamed through the showroom window as if it were a normal day, but there was nothing normal about the Manifesto. *Nothing in our future will be normal now.*

The fury of the July heat, radiated up her skirt from the narrow cobbled street of the Via Roma. There was no breeze. Her rayon slip was damp, her thighs moist and irritated. She was glad to escape the heat of the studio, but still had a twelve-block walk home. *I should have gone to Florence with Elia. I would have been with him when he read the Manifesto.*

Girard and Simona Gallo knew everything happening in their four-block area. They stood neighborhood vigil when business was slow. As Agnese approached, she slowed her pace, and smiled, flashing deep dimples. "*Buongiorno*, Signor, Signora," she said, expecting him to reach out, pinch her cheeks, and gush "*molto dolce*," as usual. There was no pinching today. The silence sliced through her. He opened the deli door and shoved his squatty little wife inside, but not before Simona looked at Agnese — sorrow and anguish in her eyes. The door hit Girard's rump as he disappeared. Agnese lifted her chin and choked back tears. Eight blocks to go.

~

The next morning Agnese dipped one knee to the floor and stepped into the pew at the Cathedral of St. John the Baptist. Over a mass of unruly, dark curls, she readjusted her black lace mantilla, a gift from Isabella, her sister in America. She placed her handbag at her feet. Renati is late, she thought. Yesterday's memory flooded back — Renati — crossing the street to avoid her. She fumbled in her pocketbook for a handkerchief. Three years ago, news came that Renati's husband had died in an auto accident. "Elia," she said that night, "We must find ways to help her. She has to find the strength to come to Mass alone, as I do. It's not easy, just as it isn't easy for you to attend synagogue alone. I want to be there for her, if she'll let me." Their friendship grew in the shadow of grief, meeting for Mass three times a week, same days, same time, same pew.

Agnese crossed her heart, and bowed her head in silent prayer. Father, give me the strength to live with Mussolini's hate for my husband. Show me how to protect him. Bless our marriage in ever-greater measures, Lord, and forgive me for asking for more. We pray for your intercession, and protection, in the days ahead. Amen.

She raised her head to see Renati Sacco looking back at her from across the aisle, two pews up. No sign of a smile. Agnese stared back. The fullness of the moment — crushing. She blinked, long and slow, and turned to face the altar. She isn't strong enough to reject what Fascism demands. I must try to understand. She won't be the last.

At the tinkle of the sanctuary bell, they stood in unison, and made the sign of the cross. "Amen." The blessing was given. She responded: "I confess to almighty God, and to you, my brothers and sisters, that I have greatly sinned . . ."

Marta De Felice, and Ilaria Como whispered in the pew behind her. She heard her name. Of course, they noticed. Renati's here, but not beside me. She thought she heard, "married to a Jew." Before the last 'Amen,' she slipped out to the street. Renati? Please God, not Renati. Wobbling atop tall, wedged shoes, on damp cobblestones, she passed solemn faces, dejected shoulders, and a sadness she had never felt in Torino. Today, I will take down that damned 'Closed' sign, and get back to business. Dear God, let us survive this.

~

She listened for Elia's footsteps on the stairs, and held out her left hand — her ring finger empty. Three years past, 1935,

[45]

Mussolini declared a national "Day of Faith." From pulpits, Italian wives were asked to lay their wedding rings "upon the altar of the Lord, for the Fatherland, for the good of Italia." Synagogues in Torino supported the "Day of Faith." Rabbi Dioli looked out over the crowd of worshippers, and intoned:

"Failing to sacrifice your wedding ring, the symbol of all you hold dear, is failing the duty you owe the homeland. A grievous failing. A selfish betrayal. Women of Italy, turn in your marital bands for the greater good of our country, and the heart of your religion. Give your gold to the Fatherland."

Italian men were not asked to give up their symbol of union. Many Jewish men in the country didn't wear the band, but Elia did. With great pride and sobriety, he deposited it into the upturned palm of Rabbi Dioli.

The tides of tragedy will swallow us, Agnese thought. Where women once walked the long cathedral aisles to receive their ring, they walked the same aisles to give it up. "I will not give them my ring, Elia. Why would I sacrifice for Fascism — my ring? I will not! You can't expect me too." His stricken face turned from her. "Look at me. What are you doing to us?" Her bones chilled. Angry at his silence.

Unmoved by his pain. "Don't ever, ever mention it again, Elia."

She left her 18k gold band inscribed EF ♥ AIF, with Father Boveri. He took her hand and led her into one of the three naves. "Agnese, we are alone here. Look," he said, as he removed a piece of loose limestone in the narrow space behind a full-sized replica of the Virgin Mary cradling her crucified son. "Place your ring here. Only you and I will know, child."

~

She had no doubt about Elia's ring. It was melted down. Used for the Fatherland to purchase a gift for Mussolini's whore, Claretta Petracci, or something equally coarse and ugly.

Agnese's ring stayed protected by the Virgin, and prominent in her prayers. "Holy Mary, Mother of God, let Mussolini receive no pleasure from the beloved ring I placed on Elia's finger, the ring he gave up in devotion to his country. Take Mussolini's power from him, Lord, and strike him impotent. Amen." Elia's footsteps brought her out of her reverie.

~

[47]

She met him at the door with the Manifesto in her hand, and flung her arms around him. "We will go to America, darling," she whispered into the softness of his neck. "We can stay with Isabella and Ignazio. They will be so happy."

He laughed, louder and higher-pitched than usual, and pushed away to look at her. "Aggy, what are you saying? You've never wanted to go to New York. We will stay here, in our home, and we will be safe."

Dinner was his favorite, a Carbonara and a bottle of Syrah from the Rhone Valley — an inferior bottle, but still, a rare treat. A jarring day deserved food to soothe the soul, but Agnese was not comforted. Holding her wine glass, her elbow propped on the table, she said, "Elia, I won't bring a child into this madness. If you insist on staying here, we will not have children." His reply was not slow in coming.

"*Amore mio.*" He grabbed her wine glass and slammed it to the table. "This is a decision we make together. No? We haven't reached madness yet. He rose, and circled the table as he spoke. My family is famous here. Our business is open. Italians hate the Manifesto and Torino is outraged."

"We will no longer be legally married, Elia. You understand that, right? You will lose your citizenship. We may lose our home. It is madness. You will not go to America. We will not have children in Italia, the church be damned."

"He's doing this to appease Hitler, Agnese," his voice low and measured. "Undo our marriage? Impossible. It's all bravado."

She straightened and stared him down. "Look at Esther and Davitt. They are shaking in fear for their babies. I'm not worried about me. It is you, Elia. You are naive. Talk is heating up. You hear it on the streets, too.

"I hear clearly enough, Aggy, and I will protect you, and our children."

"You can't protect me here in Italy. You can't protect even yourself. And Elia, tell me — where is Chiano Ruber and the other Jewish leaders of the Fascist Party? No one knows what happened to Ruber. He's gone — just gone. What do you know about that?"

~

In the years leading up to the war, after the 'sacrifice of wedding rings,' and the Manifesto, Fermi Photography did well enough, but there were changes. A Sunday stroll in the Piazza San Carlo made it impossible for Agnese to dismiss the

[49]

mumbled conversations, the foreheads nearly touching as they whispered — none too quietly — mouths shielded behind a guarding hand. A sideways glance as they passed. The occasional, unmistakable, echoes of "Aryan." Elia said he noticed nothing.

An auburn-haired, green-eyed Jew with ancient roots in modern-day Scotland, Elia's ancestors arrived in Rome in 150 A.D. He read the Manifesto every morning, every evening. With it came strong coffee, warm milk, and a buttered croissant. On his morning walk to the studio, and at the end of the day, he pulled the bed covers over his wife and laid beside her, silently reciting from memory:

Jews do not belong to the Italian race. The purely European character of the Italians would be altered by breeding with any other non-European race bearing a civilization different from the millennial civilization of the Aryans.

There was little sleep for either of them. Most nights he could see her shoulders trembling under the covers. "Aggy, amore, please don't cry."

~

Signor Gallo flung wide the door of Fermi Photography. "Have you heard, Elia? It has happened. Il Duce announced Italia has joined the war on the side of the Nazis." His hands shook as he dabbed at his pale, watery eyes with a handkerchief. "You must take care, my friend. It's not safe for you or Signora Fermi here."

"Girard," Elia said, as he placed his hands on the old man's shoulders, "remember, Grandfather Fermi was a celebrated general in the Great War. Italia reveres him. Even the Fascists are indebted to him. This is not good for your heart. Please, sit down and rest."

~

While friends slipped away in the night, with only the clothes on their backs, Agnese and Elia stayed. A small piece of paper slipped into a pocket. An address. The unspoken message: 'If you need help, come here' 'We will feed you.' 'We will hide you.' The Fermi's marriage now illegal, Elia's citizenship undone, but in Torino, there was no knock on the door, no government summons.

~

Elia, face flushed bright red, flashed the letter in front of Agnese. "The Collaborative Arts of Italy, Aggy, is giving me an award for my Calabrian coastline exhibit. Isn't that something? I'm to go to Rome. There's a dinner and a ceremony. Listen, *amore mio,* they say my photographs are 'inspired genius.' You must come with me. You haven't been to Rome for years. It's Rome, *amore mio.* It's Rome." She reached and held his face in her hands. A terrible fear gripped her chest. I can't let him see it. Her blood raced, temples throbbed. She cleared her throat to steady her voice.

"We cannot close the shop, darling. It will call attention to us. It's too risky. You go. We will tell only those we are closest to. When you return — we hang the plaque on the studio wall."

~

The Hotel Bernini-Bristol was packed. Elia washed-up and changed into dinner clothes — of which he owned none. Giacoma Landi, his photographic equipment supplier in Florence, loaned him a suit of clothing. While not fine fashion, the suit represented respectability. The fedora stayed in Torino.

From his table at the back of the ballroom, he made his way to the stage, where recipients stepped to the microphone to express their gratitude. The judge handed him a certified piece of fine quality paper, and stayed planted behind the podium. Elia did not say 'thank you.' He was the only Jew in the room.

After the ceremony, he wrapped and packed the suit, and went for a walk in the city. He neared the Triton Fountain and heard a voice behind him, "Jew, turn around." He kept walking. The voice, closer now, "Jew, turn around." Two Italian *polizia* grabbed his hands, and bound them behind him.

~

Agnese waited, sleepless. Neither reason, nor optimism could break through a broken heart. After two days, she closed the studio. After four, she traveled to Rome. The Bernini-Bristol knew nothing. The military knew nothing. At the district police station, a clerk skimmed a roster and said her husband's name was not logged. She turned to a policeman standing near, "I'm looking for my husband, a renowned photographer from Torino. He has dark red hair, green eyes, and is tall and thin. I've checked hospitals, and cannot find him. Can you help me?"

[53]

"Ah, Signora, maybe he couldn't remember the way home," he grinned, his lips crusted, and swollen under an unkempt mustache. "I will walk you through the cells. Maybe you will recognize him." He followed her as she stopped at each dirty, overcrowded cube. Prisoners stomped the floor, made hand gestures, and touched her as she came close to look at every face. She didn't feel the groping. Ignored their obscenities. She ran her fingers along the bars. He was here. They brought him here. At the end of the dank hallway, she forced herself to thank her escort, and as she did, her chin quivered. God, speak to me. Tell me what to do.

~

Enzio Grimaldi's signature was on the letter from The Collaborative Arts of Italy. Agnese traveled to the Florence headquarters. "Signor Grimaldi is away on business. So sorry, Signora." For days, she sat on the building's steps. "Signor, are you Enzio Grimaldi? No? It's a matter of life and death. He's the Chairman of The Collaborative Arts? Please, Signor!"

~

Giacamo Landi stopped by the studio, and learned that he would not get his suit back. He left with the fedora, and began his own unfruitful search. November arrived, and Giacamo offered Agnese a good price for Fermi Photography.

~

On a bright Wednesday afternoon after Mass, Agnese shared lunch with Father Boveri. Together they walked through the nave and disappeared behind the Virgin Mary. She removed the stone, and grasped the ring. Before she could get it on her finger, her knees buckled. The Father caught her, and held her in his arms until she could stand. "Father, I'll see you for breakfast in Bolzano, tomorrow."

"I'll be there, child."

~

Together, they drove to a Benedictine nunnery in South Tyrol, where Agnese became Sister Margit.

~

Isabella Iscopo Pianini pulled a letter from her mailbox. The return address was Father Boveri, her family priest in Turin. Lightheaded, her heartbeat rapid, Isabella lowered herself to the steps of her Brooklyn row house. There had been no word from her younger sister since 1937. The letter remained unopened until her brother, Ignazio, arrived that evening.

Ciao, dearest Isabella,

After all these years I can still see your fresh, smiling face, and I remember the day you left Torino for America. How I wish we could sit down and talk about the years past. That is not to be, so in the event you have not heard from Agnese since the end of the war, I must tell you what I know. In 1941, after Italy declared war on the United States, I arranged for Agnese to enter a convent in Alto Adige…

~

Ignazio traveled to the cloisters. There was no Sister Margit, no Agnese, and never had been. They let him watch the nuns as they passed on the way to prayer, but he hadn't seen his sister since a photo years ago, and hadn't seen her in person since she was thirteen years old. Mother Abbess Angella sent him to Torino's city hall. There he found Elia Fermi's name on a list of Italians who fell to the Nazis at Auschwitz-Birkenau.

Isabella Pianini and Ignazio Iscopo died without knowing the fate of Agnese.

Soul of the Departed
by
M. Carolyn Steele

The news that Gus Holland's horse was out in the middle of Main Street with a headless body roped to its saddle, emptied the Scratchin' Dog Saloon in a hurry. I went looking for the broom so I could sweep up. I didn't want to ogle a corpse without its noggin. I mean, what kinda right-thinking girl would? Everyone knows that without a head plugging up the neck, the soul of the newly departed can escape and go wandering about searching for a new mortal to inhabit.

That's what was wrong with Gus in the first place. He had two souls. Mean as a rabid skunk one minute; sweet as pie the next. Just last Sunday he came wagging a silver dollar in front of my face while I was taking my supper on the back step. Words dripped from his mouth like melted butter all over my plate of beans. Only it wasn't butter. It was spit.

I told him as how I'd admire to have that shiny dollar, but I reckoned he'd better go on upstairs to see Louise or Tolly because they'd already rouged their cheeks and wrapped wisps of hair around heated nails until it appeared watch springs were growing out their heads.

Louise had brown hair. Tolly had yellow. Mamaw liked to keep one of each, seeing as how cowboys had their preferences.

Gus looked strange for a minute when I told him Mamaw forbid me selling favors, even for a shiny dollar. His face got red and his mustache twitched. I swear his curly black hair went porcupine-straight.

Startled me so bad, I dropped my plate of beans on his boots—a pure mistake. Gus was proud of his boots—alligator skin, not cowhide—got back in Louisiana after the Rebellion. Veins popped out on either side of his neck, and he exploded like a firecracker, hissing sulfur and all. Even with her big ol' shotgun, Mamaw about never got him calmed down. Like I said, he had two souls, one good and one bad. So, it didn't surprise me Gus got himself headless.

My broom wasn't at the back door or behind the piano, which upset me considerable since sweeping was my job. That, and emptying spittoons, rubbing up whisky glasses, and running errands for Mamaw's girls. I wandered past the now deserted tables, cards and poker chips scattered, even a still-smoldering cigar. Being the middle of the week, the saloon had been peaceful until Gus came along.

It wasn't likely I'd left the broom on the front boardwalk. What could I do, but check out the possibility? I heard 'em before I ever pushed through the swinging doors. Everyone remarking on how, without no head, Gus never looked so good before. That sort of nonsense.

Gus and his twin brother, Harold, were nice lookin' fellas. Strange thing was, Gus had eyes dark as night and Harold's was cornflower blue. Mamaw said it was plain as the nose on your face, the twin's ma had bedded two men the same night. And Mamaw ought to know about such things.

My broom wasn't nowhere in sight, not laying on the boardwalk nor leaning against the wall. I would hate to lose that broom. It wasn't one of those Mexican-made brooms fashioned out of a crooked piece of mesquite wood. Mamaw got it at the mercantile just for me. It had a smooth handle, painted red. Once in a while, I'd sweep the steps and lean it against the hitching post while I sat and watched folks mosey in and out of the only mercantile in Muddy Springs.

In case I'd left the broom at the railing, I was going to have to look in the direction of all the commotion, whether I wanted to or not. It was then I couldn't help noticing Gus's big white stallion, snorting and throwing his head, stomping his right hoof, near digging a hole in the ground. He purely didn't like a dead man sitting on his back, even if it was Gus. Horses are like that. They can smell death and won't go near it.

Not long ago, one of the boys told about a Texas Ranger being chased by Comanches. He laid his horse down and slit its throat. Those Indian ponies stiff-legged and wouldn't go near the Ranger, who was squatting in a pool of blood, waiting for 'em. That stallion of Gus's was acting just like the smell of death was driving him stiff-legged, too.

I didn't want to look, but my eyes took on a mind of their own. I clamped my mouth shut tight so Gus's evil soul couldn't find its way into my throat. At least that was my intention. But the sight of a headless body punched the air right out of me.

"Oh!"

Gus was trussed up tighter than a cotton bale, arms pulled close to his body, hands and reins secured to the pommel with double knots, and boots jammed in the stirrups. And, just to make sure his feet didn't go flopping out of the boots, a rope had been passed under the stallion to tie both ankles together.

Even with the horse shaking his mane and rabbit-hopping, Gus sat poker straight in the saddle. Oh, he swayed a tad one way or another, causing almost as much commotion as when he'd got drunk and tried to hang his brother from the saloon rafters. Mamaw had to get the shotgun then, too.

Berchard, our piano player, struggled with the knots, making to undo them, and cussed a blue streak. Old Jake tried to calm the stallion, holding him by the bit-ring, crooning sweet words, and rubbing a beer-sopped apron over the horse's nose to dull the smell of death. The rest of the boys hooted and hollered, making bets on how long Gus could stay in the saddle before he took a tumble.

"Annie, bring that huntin' knife from under the bar." Mamaw grabbed my arm and shoved me back toward the saloon doors. She handled any trouble that found its way to Muddy Springs since Sheriff Adams strangled on a wad of tobacco. Most folks said it was because he was partial to Mexican leaves, and they cross tobacco with chili peppers.

Nobody wanted the chore of keeping things calm, so Mamaw took over. Lawlessness was bad for business, she said. We all knew she wouldn't hesitate one whit to pull the trigger on her shotgun should the occasion demand it.

The rusty knife, blade half long as my arm, wasn't anywhere around. Old Jake called it his Indian-killing weapon, but I expect it was nothing more than an old butcher knife. I settled for Jake's pocketknife, the one he used for popping corks.

I hurried for the front porch when I heard it plain as day––a creak in the floorboards. The saloon was empty, excepting for the dust motes dancing in the beams of sunlight shining through the back door, which I must have left open when I looked for my broom. Another groan of boards, softer this time, came from upstairs and then a latch, like a door closing easy.

Probably one of the cowboys, most likely Three-Toes, talked one of the girls into a roll while Mamaw was outside. It was cheaper that way, paying direct instead of going through Mamaw. She'd be mad when she found out.

I marched out front, lips squeezed tight. Someone told one of the boys to run for Doc Harper and I wondered what for. It wasn't like you could fix what was wrong with Gus.

Shading my eyes against the sight, I held the knife out for Berchard. He flailed one hand toward me while holding onto the stirrup, and though I leaned out from the top step, our arms weren't long enough.

"Thunderation, Li'l Annie," Mamaw said. "Get on down there. Ain't nothin' gonna bite you." She was frowning, and that meant she was serious. Mamaw said frowning set wrinkles in a woman's face. In her line of business, that meant retiring to another line of work, like washing clothes. Serving up whiskey and sporting gals ain't nearly so demanding as laundry.

I wanted to warn her to keep her mouth shut, or she might get another soul living inside her, but then I'da put my own self at risk.

Berchard took the knife, bent down, and went to sawing the rope. The stirrup swung loose. It was then I got a good look at the boots Gus was wearing. My mouth dropped wide open again.

"Berchard," I said and pointed to the scruffiest boots I ever saw.

"Get out the way, Li'l Annie. I'm doin' the best I can." He stretched and cut through the reins holding Gus's hands to the pommel and stepped back.

By now all of Muddy Creek had gathered around—folks from the mercantile, and the barber shop, and fellas from down at the blacksmith's. It got real quiet, nobody wanting to be the one to drag Gus out of the saddle.

The stallion solved that problem. He pulled loose of Old Jake and reared.

Just like that, Gus hit the ground so hard he stirred a layer of dirt and lay sprawled out in what would have been face down. Mrs. Russell, from the mercantile, screamed and fainted, landing right next to him.

"Mercy sakes," Mamaw said.

"Look at them flies," Short Billy said. "Whew." He snorted and went to swatting at a swarm of big ol' horseflies that had followed Gus to the ground.

Doc came running down the boardwalk and pushed through the crowd. "Let me through. Everybody get back." He saw Mrs. Russell almost on top a headless man and stopped dead in his tracks.

"Doc . . . Mrs. Russell only swooned. She's all right." Mamaw's rosy silk skirt crinkled as she gathered it up and stepped off the boardwalk, lifting the hem out of the dirt. "Berchard, you and Billy tote her over to the mercantile." The flies fought their way back to Gus once Short Billy let off fanning the air.

"Now," said Mamaw, "when was the last time any of you boys saw Gus? With his head on, that is. Possum, what about you?"

Possum was Gus's sometimes friend. He was half Comanche but right now he was pale as sand. Indians were superstitious about things like headless bodies. "Sunday, maybe so."

"Doc, how long has Gus been dead, you reckon?"

Doc grunted as he got down on one knee, lifted Gus's hand, and let it drop to the ground. "Well, he's floppy. Past the stiff stage. By the smell, I'd say, maybe three days." He motioned to the boys. "One of you fellas help turn him over."

No one moved. Three-Toes stepped off the boardwalk. "Bunch of sissy-babies. He's dead. Can't hurt nobody now." Three-Toes come out of the Civil War without a couple of toes he was natural born with, so I guess missing a body part didn't seem odd to him.

I wondered who was upstairs with one of the girls if it wasn't Three-Toes. I looked around and saw Louise with an arm around Tolly, sniffing and clutching a hand to her bosom.

"Somebody needs to ride out and tell Harold about his brother." Mamaw nodded to Possum.

"Um, Harold gone to Mexico, round up cattle," Possum said, looking a little less pale. "Gus's father die awhile back. Father leave ranch to oldest son, Harold. Like in Good Book. Gus mad about that."

Everybody knew that after Harold got born, his ma labored on a full thirty minutes before Gus peeped through. Those brothers never did like each other much.

"Reckon one of them Comanches done this?" Three-Toes was swatting flies so the doc could look for bullet holes. "I hear the Rangers been trying to drive them up to the territories."

Possum shook his head. "Huh uh. Comanche no do this. Indians take scalp, not whole head."

Mamaw tapped her chin with one finger. "Possum's right. Seems to me more likely Harold's doing. After all, Gus did try to hang him."

The smell coming from Gus was near intolerable. Mamaw pulled a hankie from her bosom.

"Anything else, Doc?"

"Nope, don't seem to be any other injuries." He stood up and pulled out his handkerchief, too. "I'll just put cause of death as loss of head, clean down to the shoulders. Though I can't figure how come there's not more blood. That shirt should have been soaked to the pants. The body's got a bucket of blood." He wrinkled his face just like he'd eaten a green persimmon. "Best get Gus in the ground soon."

"It ain't Gus," I said. His souls would have taken residence somewhere else by now, so it was safe to say my piece. Everyone took to staring at me like I was crazy.

"Nonsense, Li'l Annie." Mamaw huffed up the steps. "Of course that's Gus. Looks just like him. Ain't that Gus's plaid shirt? It's a tad bloody now, but he's been wearing it for the last month." Mamaw flipped her hand. "Turn him over again. See if his initials ain't on the belt. I believe I recollect seeing that."

[67]

Three-Toes stood and gave the body a mighty shove with his foot. It rolled, and, sure enough, "G.H." was carved in the leather.

"It ain't Gus." I could feel it in my bones. "Look at those boots. Gus would never wear plain ol' boots. Why would he, when he has good alligator ones?"

Three-Toes stepped over the body and gave it another shove to roll it back. He whistled. "Why, Lil Annie's right."

Rolling the body back and forth had loosened things up and here come a red stick working out of Gus's shirt collar.

A chill washed right over me. "My . . . my broom!" I could hardly talk.

Doc and the boys scrambled to pull the broom handle from the back of Gus's shirt. The straw bottom was whacked off.

"Guess that's why Gus was sitting so straight in the saddle," Short Billy mumbled and went back to fanning flies.

"It ain't Gus," I repeated, mad at whoever had done such a thing to my broom.

Mamaw frowned again for the second time in one day. Lifting her skirts, she left the boardwalk and walked around to where she could peer down Gus's shirt collar. The shirt was buttoned wrong and the right side of the collar flopped over the neck hole. "Possum, I suppose you ought to ride back down the road, see if you can find where Gus lost his head. Hate to bury anyone missin' a part."

Tolly's lip-quivering let loose and she started wailing.

"Mercy sakes, Tolly, what's got into you? You've seen a dead person before." Mamaw sighed. "I'll allow this might be the first time without a top-knot."

"Gus . . . was . . . gonna . . . marry me," Tolly blubbered. "Gonna . . . take me . . . out to his ranch." Tears rolled down her checks, and her body shook so hard the red feathers stuck in her curls quivered like they was taking flight.

I stared at her. Some cowpoke's always asking one of the girls to marry 'um. They didn't never mean it, once they sober up. Besides, why would she want to marry a two-souled man?

"Tolly, you always was a simple-minded thing." Mamaw clucked her tongue. "When did Gus ask you to marry him?"

"Last Sunday night." Tolly sniffed and lifted the hem of her dress clean up to her nose and blew.

Mamaw looked at me and back to Tolly. "How late? 'cause I chased Gus off around supper time."

Tolly quit sniffling and commenced twisting the hem of her skirt. She'd clearly gone against Mamaw's rules.

"The moon was up. Midnight?"

"Goodness." I couldn't help asking, "Was he drunk?"

"Maybe." Tolly smoothed her skirt down. "Just a little."

"How come you believed him, then?"

"He left his boots under my bed. Said he had things to do, but that would prove he would come back."

"So you let him under the covers?"

Tolly nodded. "Gus said he loved me. And now . . . ." The corners of her mouth pulled down and she wailed, "Now, I ain't never . . . gonna . . . get married."

"That explains the boots," Mamaw said. "Louise, you take Tolly upstairs 'til she can quit her blubberin'." She turned to Whiskers, the barber. He did all the hair cutting, tooth pulling, and burying for Muddy Springs. "Don't reckon you'll have to do much to make Gus presentable. Might put a clean shirt on him."

"Tote 'im to the barber shop, boys." Whiskers took both legs and directed Three-Toes to grab one arm and Short Billy, the other. "I got a pine box waitin' for an occupant."

"Wait!" A clean shirt. That was it.

Mamaw sighed. "What now?"

"Gus was fussy about his appearances." I pointed at the body. "I never once saw him with his buttons fastened wrong like that. Doc, you said there should be more blood."

Three-Toes, Short Billy, and Whiskers stopped dragging Gus, looked down, and nodded at the peculiarity.

"That shirt wasn't on that body when its head went missin'."

"Aww, Annie," Three-Toes said. "Who'd wanna dress up a body missin' its head?"

"Someone who wants us to think this is Gus. That's who!"

Short Billy dropped the arm he was holding and the body sagged. "If this ain't Gus, who is it?"

The awfullest screams from the saloon stopped our speculations and everyone rushed to get through the swinging doors at the same time. Pushing from behind, Mamaw broke the jam.

"Get my shotgun, Berchard!" she shouted.

Louise met us at the top of the stairs, screaming, pointing down the hall. We all near trampled each other to get to

Tolly's room. She stood frozen just inside the door, mouth open, but nothing coming out.

Gus, in his stocking feet, straddled the windowsill.

At first we was all speechless. Then, Mamaw said, "Well, if it ain't Gus, come back from the dead."

"Dark eyes snapping, Gus glared at us and, then, Tolly. "Ain't askin' again. Where's my boots? They ain't under the bed, ain't in the wardrobe, and ain't in the trunk."

Hiccupping, she pointed to the bed. "Under . . . under . . . them pillows. Didn't want 'um sto-stolen."

Berchard handed Mamaw the shotgun. You could see Gus was torn between jumping or going for his boots.

"Who's down in the street, wearin' your clothes?" Mamaw cradled the gun in her arm.

"How should I know?" Gus turned his evil-soul stare on Mamaw. "Give my clothes to a stranger, and the ingrate stole my horse. Must be him."

"Ain't no stranger. It's your brother, Harold. Ain't it?"

"Prove it," Gus said and laughed, a deep hee-haw laugh just like Harold's.

It took all the boys to wrestle him off the windowsill and down to the jail.

Later that night, when the saloon should have been bustling, it was empty except for Old Jake, Berchard, and us girls. Possum hadn't come back. Not knowing for certain who was headless, the cowpokes got spooked and went home. Turns out they were more superstitious than Comanches.

I was piqued, 'cause no one remarked on how smart I'd been. Still, if Gus hadn't come looking for his alligator boots, everything woulda been fine with the cowpokes thinking it was him, and Mamaw wouldn't be frowning.

"This ain't good for business," she said. "Trouble is . . . most likely, Gus is right. Without a head, we can't prove that was Harold we buried this afternoon. No telling how long it's gonna take for the boys to get thirsty again."

"Or lonesome," Louise sighed.

The Indian-killing knife was still missing, just like Harold's head. Over to the jail house we could hear that hee-haw laugh, now and again, and I reckoned one thing wasn't missing. Harold's soul.

My First Cattle Drive
(Excerpt from Runt – A Cowboy's Story)
by
Jim Laughter

My old pa was a drover. He set 'is saddle twelve hours a day drivin' cattle up the Santa Fe, Western, and Chisholm Trails from New Mexico and Texas to the railheads north in Kansas and Missouri. Dependin' on the trail they was drivin', sometimes he'd go as far as Nebraska and Wyomin'. It didn't matter how harsh the weather conditions was, he just rode right on through'em. He suffered dangers from hostile Injuns and rustlers, twisters and sandstorms, drought, flood, and famine. Weren't no kind'a pestilence, natural or otherwise could stop a herd'a beef once them cowboys got'em started on the trail.

I'll never forget the day they brung Pa home in the back of a buckboard. His right leg was all shot up and busted from where they'd been in a fight in the panhandle with a pack'a renegade Comanche out to stir up trouble. Pa said the Injuns snuck up on 'em in the middle of the night and tried to stampede the herd. Comanches are known to do that, so I wouldn't put it past 'em. Truth be told, they consider the Santa Fe their territory so they demand a toll from anybody usin' it, whether it be a cattle drive or settlers just tryin' to get from one place to 'tuther. He said they shot 'is horse right out from under 'im. Said the arrow went through 'is leg and kilt 'is horse, causin' the critter to fall on top of 'im and smash 'is leg a'gin the ground. He said he thought he was a goner fer sure that time but the other boys pulled 'im out and patched 'im up.

Times was sure lean that winter 'cause Pa couldn't ride or hardly even walk with is bandy leg all sore and busted up. It's a good thing he taught me and my little brother Jimmy how to hunt rabbits and other game when we was just young'uns or we'd a starved slap to death that winter fer sure. Deer and antelope was scarce in our part'a the country, but ever now and then we'd bag us a buck or white tail doe and it'd hold us over fer a while. There ain't nothin' better'n a hank of venison jerky on a cold winter night.

I remember askin' Pa one fall when he come home after a drive to Kansas City what it took to be a cowboy. I was thinkin' I might take up the trade when I got a few more years under my belt, even though Ma wanted me to stay in school and make somethin' of myself. But I didn't figure I'd stay in school much after turnin' fourteen or so. After all, if'n a man can't make it on 'is own when he's half-growed, what good's a bunch'a schoolin'?

Anyhow, I asked Pa what it took to be a cowboy, figurin' I'd sit 'is saddle once he couldn't do it no more. He looked me square in my eyeball and said, "Well sir." Pa always called ever'body sir, regardless how young or how old they was. And you can bet your good boots when me and Jimmy spoke to 'im, we damn sure called 'im sir too if'n we didn't wanna catch the back of 'is hand upside our heads.

He said, "Well sir. First, you gotta be smarter'n the horse you're ridin'. Second, you gotta be tougher'n the saddle you're settin'. And thirdly, you gotta shoot straighter'n the other sum'bitch shootin' back at ya."

I reckon that was some of the best advice my old pa ever give me, 'specially the part about shootin' straighter'n the other sum'bitch shootin' back at me. I've used that little bit'a wisdom more'n once in the twenty-somethin' years I've been ridin' the trail. It ain't that I go lookin' fer trouble. It's just that trouble always catches up to me no matter how hard I try to avoid it.

I remember once when I was spendin' a night or two in Abilene, Kansas after a particular hard drive up the Chisholm. Me and a few'a the boys was takin' up space at the Spur 'N Saddle sippin' rye and swappin' lies when fer no reason whatsoever a young feller standin' at the bar must'a took offense at somethin' or 'tuther I said. We all had our eighty dollars gold coin in our pockets so I don't know why that wild-eyed knot-head from the Oklahoma Territory decided to single me out. It weren't like I took advantage of 'is sister or nothin'. He just either had a mean streak in 'im or he was too drunk to know the difference. He just picked me out'ta the crowd to get 'is feathers ruffled with and slung a shot across the saloon like he didn't have no better sense.

Anyhow, there I set with the boys mindin' my own business when this yea-hoo decided to draw down on me. I didn't know he was shootin' at me at first 'cause 'is bullet ricocheted off across the saloon and busted a mirror hangin' on the wall next to the stairs goin' up to the girly rooms. Then he pointed 'is *pistolla* right at me, 'is hand waverin' side to side like he was tryin' to take aim at cat-tails blowin' in the wind down by the creek. Then he called me a name I'd ruther not repeat. Without even blinkin' twice, he fired a second shot that busted the glass right out'ta my hand and set me down hard on the floor. We was all surprised the bullet didn't hit Slim Jerkins sittin' there beside me. But old Slim's so damn skinny you can't hardly see 'im if he's standin' sideways to ya.

Well sir, there I set on the floor when I seen this cowboy take aim at me agin', so I pulled my Pa's old .44 out'ta my holster. Even though the boy wasn't shootin' straight, he was gettin' mighty close to puttin' out my liver and lights, and I wasn't 'bout to give 'im another free shot, not at me anyhow. But I knew I didn't wanna kill the kid either. I sure as hell didn't want'ta stand trial fer murder in no cow town, regardless if it was self-defense or not.

Rememberin' what my Pa said about shootin' straighter'n the sum'bitch shootin' back at me, I leveled that old Colt on the chair next to me and took good aim at 'is shootin' shoulder. Dropped the sum'bitch like a cow patty hittin' soft dirt. When the smoke cleared and I was able to scramble up to my feet, I sauntered over to the boy and looked down on 'im to see if I knew 'im from anywhere. His face didn't ring no bells and none of the boys knew who he was, so we just waited fer the sheriff to show up. It didn't take long fer the

[79]

barkeep and a few other folks standin' around to clear the air fer me and I was able to go about my business, which meant I packed my saddle bag and bedroll and shagged my ass right on out'ta town.

I reckon that was about the closest I ever come to gettin' myself kilt fer no good reason at all, not that I didn't have a few scrapes along the way that I should'a steered clear of. In my twenty-somethin' years on the trail, I've been chased by wild Injuns, stampeded more'n once, and even got caught up in a bank robbery when I went in to change a twenty-dollar gold coin so's I could buy supplies fer the trail. Flung myself out an open win'der onto the wood sidewalk to avoid gettin' my money took. Them robbers got clean away but not with my earnin's they didn't. I even damn near got run over by a stagecoach once. I still ain't never figured out how that happened but the fact is it missed me by a frog's hair and scared hell out'ta both me and my horse. Course, I only stand a smidgen over five feet tall in my stockin' feet, just a might taller if'n I'm wearin' my hat, but surely that damn crazy stagecoach driver could'a seen my horse.

But I'm gettin' ahead of myself. I was fixin' to tell ya 'bout the day I turned sixteen year old. I quit goin' to school when I was fourteen. Didn't figure I needed schoolin' past the eighth grade anyhow, and I could do my figures and letters good 'nuff to get by. Instead, I took odd jobs on ranches and such helpin' dig wells and build fences, wranglin' cattle durin' brandin' season -- that sort'a thing. Course, I watched after Ma and Jimmy when Pa was away on a drive.

Well sir, Pa come home about a week before my sixteenth birthday. We had us a little spread just outside Ft. Worth, Texas. It weren't much to brag about, just a couple hundred acres of Texas prairie and scrub oak, but it was our'n and ever thing on it was paid fer. Pa didn't owe a nickel to nobody, and he sure as hell pounded that philosophy into me and Jimmy. He'd say if'n you don't owe nobody nothin', ain't nobody can take what's your'n.

Anyhow, Pa set me down on the front porch and asked me what I planned to do from then on. I weren't smart enough to know he was fixin' to kick my ass out the house and make me start earnin' my own way. I told 'im I didn't rightly know what I intended to do, that I figured I'd just go on workin' odd jobs fer ranchers in the territory till somethin' else come along.

So on my sixteenth birthday, me and Pa stood in the front room'a our house and we was facin' the door. Pa draped 'is right arm over my shoulder and said, "Son, today you are a man."

I said, "Yes sir."

He said, "You're sixteen year old today."

I said, "Yes sir."

"That's the 'xact same age I was when I set out on my own."

I didn't answer 'im that time, although I prob'ly should'a. Fer some reason I didn't figure this conversation was gonna end with nothin' I liked.

Pa pulled me close to 'im, 'is strong right arm crushin' me a'gin 'im. Then he said, "You see that front door right there?"

I said, "Yes sir."

He said, "Hit it."

Course my mama cried and said I was too young to be settin' out on my own, but Pa weren't havin' no part of it. He said if'n a man could set around on 'is ass and do nothin', he could set 'is ass in a saddle and make a livin'.

I'm thinkin' that was the last full conversation I had with my Pa that year. What I didn't know was durin' that first week of 'im bein' home, he'd arranged fer me to join a drive movin' a herd'a longhorns up the Chisholm Trail to the railhead in Abilene, Kansas where they'd be loaded on a train to St. Louis, Missouri then further east to New York and other cities I didn't figure I'd ever see. He'd used some of 'is drive money to buy me a strong young mare to ride and even geared her out with a good used saddle and bedroll. Hell, he even bought me a set of chaps and a brand new ropin' rope.

I already had a purty good hat but Pa figured a man settin' out on the trail fer the first time needed a new one. He even give me a fair-to-middlin' Colt .45 pistol complete with cartridge belt. And when I climbed up on my horse fer the first time, I found a good used Winchester rifle in the saddle scabbard. Pa didn't leave nothin' to chance when it come to bein' prepared fer the trail. He said he give me the wherewithal to protect myself and what's mine and now it was up to me to make good fer myself. Only thing he told me was, "Stand yer ground, boy. Keep your eyes and ears open and yer mouth shut. Don't be a smart-ass, and ever thing else will work itself out."

So there I set on my own horse with a brand new wide-brim atop my head and all deck out in new leather chaps, prouder'n a school girl who made it to graduation with her virginity intact. I believe Pa was proud'a me in 'is own way but he weren't about to show it. He was a funny old cuss when it come to showin' emotion or affection with us boys. Then right outta the blue he'd grab our mama up in 'is arms and kiss her full on the mouth right out in public. I think he did it just to embarrass me and Jimmy. Mama always laughed and giggled when he done it, so I reckon they had their own little games they liked to play.

First day I showed up at the Murray place fer the drive, I was green and then some about how a cattle drive worked. I'd been workin' the ranches around our place fer the past couple'a years, helpin' with brandin' and such, but a drive is a differ'nt story altogether. I figured the drive would consist'a old Mr. Murray and 'is boys from the ranch – fellers I already knew and was on fairly friendly terms with. I had no way'a knowin' the cowboys Murray brung in fer the drive was a different breed'a wrangler, and Pa sure as hell didn't fill me in on it. Them boys eyeballed me like I was spare ribs at a barbeque when I rode into camp. They was saddle-tough and leather-skinned like nothin' I'd ever seen before. I could tell right off they weren't no haywire outfit. I didn't know whether to turn tail and skedaddle out'ta there or pretend I weren't nervous as a long-tail cat in room full'a rockin' chairs.

I remembered Pa tellin' me to stand my ground and ever thing would work itself out. So I rode real slow into camp, them cowboys watchin' me and me watchin' them. I figured they never seen a brand new hat before, much less one set atop a sixteen year old kid with nary a whisker on 'is face.

Anyway, I spotted Mr. Murray squatted down alongside a campfire pourin' the blackest coffee I ever seen into an old bent up tin cup. One of the boys nudged 'im and nodded toward me. He stood up just as I reached the fire. He was taller and leaner than I remembered from two summers back. His face was old and crackled from the sun, and 'is hands was big and leather clad with work gloves. By the look on 'is face, I didn't figure he recognized me from helpin' fix the fence row on 'is south range.

"You the Sender boy?"

"Yes sir."

You can bet your good boots I remembered to call 'im sir. If'n he was anything like my Pa, I didn't want 'im snatchin' me down off my saddle, not in front'a all them other cowboys anyway.

"First name's Jacob but most folks just call me Jake."

I ain't got no idea why I set there on that horse like I didn't have no better sense. Mr. Murray he just stood there cup in hand lookin' up at me. He must'a thought I figured I was a prince or somethin' settin' there lookin' down on 'em. Truth is, I was scared clean off my tin-type and didn't know whether to get down or turn tail and shag ass out'ta there.

"You just gonna sit there, boy, or get down and stay a while?"

A couple'a the boys sittin' around the campfire kind'a snickered, knowin' full well how nervous I was.

"Maybe one of us or'ta take 'im over to the bunkhouse and tuck 'im in fer the night," one of 'em said.

"Hell, he don't look big 'nuff to throw a shad'er," another said. "I reckon that hat's the biggest thang 'bout this little runt."

Now, I could tell them boys was only pokin' fun at me, seein' as'ta how I'd rid right into their camp and set there like

[86]

a bump on a log. Truth is, I found it kind'a amusin' myself. Funny thing is, that was the very minute I got my name, right there by that campfire. From that very day them boys called me Runt and it's stuck to me my whole life. I reckon standin' just taller'n a jackrabbit in flat shoes will do that to a feller.

Runt Sender, that's me. You'd a thought I would'a took offense at it. But fact is, I kind'a liked it. It showed me them boys weren't gonna be all bad, no matter how rough and rugged they looked on the outside. I could tell right off they was gonna treat me good. Oh, I figured they'd tease me some, me bein' so young and all. I remember my Pa tellin' me once how new hands are broke in on their first drive, so I didn't figure it would be any different fer me. They'd prob'ly send me out lookin' fer cows with three ears and two tails, knowin' full well them cows don't exist. And I'd catch the midnight watch more'n my fair share once we got out on the drive.

Some boys would complain about ridin' dead man watch but I'd heard Pa tell Ma one time that the reason the new hands ride dead man is because that's when the cattle are asleep and there's less likelihood'a trouble. That is if'n a bunch of Comanche don't take a notion to sneak into the herd. But them times was few and far between. I'd let on like I didn't know that little tidbit'a information so them boys could have their fun. I figured I'd learn better that way. After all, cowboys can be a might touchy sometimes if'n they think you're tryin' to pull the wool over their eyes. I'd play along with'em and be the butt of their jokes. I didn't figure it would kill me and might even make me a friend or two.

Well, I'm gettin' ahead of myself tellin' this story, and damn if it ain't gettin' cold settin' out here on this prairie all by my lonesome. Reckon I'll toss another stick'a wood or two, maybe even a buffalo chip on this here campfire and roll out my bedroll and try to catch a couple hours shut-eye. That is if I can find me a patch'a ground that ain't littered with rocks. Trail can be hard on a cowboy, 'specially after a drive and he's tryin' to get back home in one piece with 'is poke and 'is scalp. I'll be a little more spry in the mornin' and we'll pick this tale up after I've throwed a cup'a coffee or two in my eyes.

This short episode is only the opening paragraphs of a book that will be published in 2016 titled Runt – A Cowboy's Story. It will be a collection of stories told by Runt Sender in 19th Century first-person western dialect. He'll go gold prospecting, railroading, get lost in the desert, and have several other wonderful adventures. Watch for updates at Jim's website www.jimlaughter.com.

The Legend of Shorty Mack
by
Michael Koch

William "Shorty" Mack and his fellow cutthroats entered Anderson and Sons General Store at Caldwell, Kansas to pick up supplies. They had been on the scout for several days looking for an easy take, possibly a bank. Inside the store, a few locals sat at a table drinking Arbuckle coffee. The morning air was cool for early October 1890.

Mack had heard that the city of Caldwell was a wild town, especially when cowboys from Texas arrived from their cattle drives. He wasn't mistaken. Some of the cowboys still in town from a long hard trip through the Indian Nations to Kansas, were ready to let loose and have some fun.

Square-jawed Henry Burrow, one of Mack's boys, glanced toward a homely looking woman sitting at a table all alone. He strolled over to strike up a conversation. "What's your name, honey?"

Henry took off his dusty cowboy hat, then licked three fingers on his right hand and attempted to smooth back a few strands of unkempt hair that had fallen over his pocked-marked face. His broad grin exposed several missing frontal teeth.

The girl leaned forward, smiled and exclaimed, "My name is Squirrel-tooth Annie…I'm five dollars for the night if you want me." Her grin exposed her buck-teeth.

"Oh, I see why you're called Squirrel-tooth Annie." He chuckled as the other men took notice and began to laugh.

Gerald "Crazy" Clark, the third party of the gang, walked over to their table, his spurs clanging with each step. He scratched a weeks' worth of whiskers. Taking a seat at a table he stated, "Howdy Miss, do you have any friends for the rest of us?"

Clark's body odor caused Annie to lean back on her wooden chair. She turned her head, catching her breath. "I think I can find some more ladies for the lot of you, but you'll have to clean up a bit."

"Good." Clark stood up and placed his right hand on his holster, which exposed his .44 caliber Colt Army revolver. He pulled his wide-brimmed hat down slightly, shading his dark brown eyes. "I'll tell the rest of the boys as I suspect we'll be staying a spell."

Clark slowly walked to the counter of the store where Mack was talking to the clerk of the establishment. He leaned closer to Mack's left ear and whispered, "I think we've got our entertainment lined up for the night."

Mack moved backward and grinned slightly. "Good," he exclaimed.

Pulling away from his position at the counter, the desperado glanced over at the table where the "lady of the night" and Burrow were jawing. Seeing all was well for the evening's activities; he told his partner and the whores, "I'm glad your gals are willing to show us a good time…I need some rest and relaxation after our long ride."

"Where you cowboys from?" The clerk scratched his long gray beard as he took a swig from a bottle of cold beer at the bar. Patches of white foam formed on the whiskers around his mouth.

Mack focused his steel-grey eyes at the clerk, frowning at his question. Pausing a few seconds, he took in a deep breath and explained, "Well sir, we're from Indian Territory…how 'bout you?" He chuckled as he suspected the inquisitive stranger had lived in Caldwell all his life.

"Well sir, I'm originally from Kentucky…came here in 78. Name's Homer Brewer. I've run this store since the early part of '85, as I enjoy the community and my job immensely."

"Good, then keep your questions to yourself and you'll enjoy it more." He placed the bottle on the bar and wiped the drops of beer from his beard with his sleeve.

"Isn't that the truth, brother?" Gerald laughed out loud. He pulled a 10-inch knife from his waistband and began to scratch his week's long whiskers with the dull side, glaring and grinning at the clerk.

"I'm sorry mister…I didn't mean anything." Brewer's hands began to quiver as he gulped and paused, "just friendly talk, mister."

The clerk was noticeably in fear for his life; his hands continued to shake as he drew a bottle of beer up to his lips. He pulled a red handkerchief from the back pocket of his old dusty pants and wiped small droplets of sweat that formed on his eyebrows.

Mack noticed a silver cigar stand on the counter top with several types of smokes. Reaching to pull one out, he put the stogie up to his nostrils and inhaled its aroma. "I'll take one of these, how much?"

The clerk, still frightened, gulped again and said, "It's on the house."

"Well, partner, that's mighty nice of you. We may stay here longer if all the folks in town are as nice and friendly as you." Smiling broadly, Mack grabbed the entire lot of cigars and passed them out to his companions.

Then out the front door they went and strolled over to the Meyer Hotel. Dust blew down the street from strong gusty winds. Dark clouds foretold that storms were arriving.

Upon entering the hotel the trio glanced about at the few well-dressed customers conversing about the lobby. Mack approached the front desk and asked the clerk, "Do you have a room available for me and my men?"

"Yes sir, how many nights."

"Well that depends! Lets' go on the notion that we'll be here at least a couple of days."

The clerk gulped as he looked directly into the stranger's sullen eyes.

"Okay." The elderly gentleman turned the registration book around for Mack and his men to sign. They made their marks with an 'X.'

"How much does it cost?" one of Mack's boys asked.

"Well, for the two days it'll be five dollars."

Mack reached into his dirty pants and pulled out a few silver dollars, checking his change he placed a five dollar piece on the counter.

The clerk gazed in amazement. "Thank you, sir." He reached for room key 303. "This is a rather large room with three beds and fresh sheets, just right for you gentlemen."

The dusty men clomped up the squeaky stairs to their room. They decided first, to bathe, as the lady of the night had requested. An uncommon practice for them. They found the washroom at the end of the hall and each paid a quarter for warm water, soap and a scrub brush.

Meanwhile, Brewer had composed himself enough to walk down a block to the marshal's office. Upon entering the office he noticed Deputy Milt Sanders sitting with his boots propped up on the desk. His feet were twitching a little causing his fancy spurs to jingle like music.

"Where's the marshal?" Brewer exclaimed, struggling to catch his breath.

Realizing something was up the deputy placed his feet on the floor, adjusted his posture in his chair, and spit a stream of tobacco into a rusty spittoon, resting on the floor nearby.

"What's the matter, Brewer?" he said, stretching his arms and folding them behind his head.

"Well there's three strangers in town...they're sure mean lookin' fellows and one of them took several of my finest cigars without paying for them."

"You don't say!" Deputy Sanders leaned forward. "Marshal, oh marshal," he yelled towards the jail cell area. A slight commotion was audible in a backroom; where cells for prisoners were located.

Marshal David Meadows entered the front of the office. Considered a hard-nosed lawman, he took no guff from anyone. He stood six-foot tall and had a large turned-down black mustache, chewed tobacco, consumed whiskey, and occasionally gambled at the local saloons. A single man, he often took up and was seen around town with a local widow. Being no different than most cowboys in town, the lawman accepted the local whores and allowed them in town, provided they didn't cause trouble. During the past several years many towns in Kansas had problems with local hotels and saloon keepers who allowed whores to entertain the cowboys that migrated to their towns each year.

The sheriff was quickly appraised by his deputy of the clerk's accusations, along with a description of the new strangers in town. He pulled a plug of tobacco from his front vest pocket, gnawed off a wad and worked it around in his mouth. Tipping his hat back from shading his eyes, he said. "Well, let's talk a spell"---"How well armed are these men?"

The deputy stood up to let his boss sit in his battered desk chair. Looking down he shuffled over several wanted posters.

"Well, Marshal...they seemed well armed for trouble." Brewer scratched his head, settling his large butt on the edge of the marshal's desk.

Meadows pulled a cheap cigar from his vest. Striking a match along his britches, he held the flame to the cigar. Brewer puffed the stogie to life. "Well, we'll just have to locate these boys to find out what they're up to. Meanwhile, if you come into contact with them again do what they ask to keep them calm."

"Okay." The noticeably shaken clerk rose from the corner of the marshal's desk, and swiftly walked out the front door. The marshal leaned back in his chair and winked at his deputy.

Meanwhile in their motel room, Mack and his boys prepared for a night of frolic. They ordered corn beef on rye sandwiches, mashed potatoes and corn, with beers to wash down their chow and appease their hunger. Later that night three unsavory women arrived for the late night entertainment. Overall the group was relatively quiet, staying in their room throughout the night.

As the morning's sun rose, brilliant rays of red lit the sky. The city streets were covered with wind-blown dust. No rain had fallen overnight, but lightning flashed in the distance sky.

Life appeared normal as people strolled around town doing their daily business. Most had covered their faces with anything they could find to keep the dust from getting in their mouths.

A local stagecoach from Topeka, Kansas, was scheduled to arrive around eleven in the morning. Weekly, a pair of well-dressed heavily armed guards escorted a shipment of cash to the First State Bank in town.

The marshal met the stagecoach as it pulled up to the bank, right on time. He helped the guards down from atop the stagecoach, where they'd guarded the money bags, four in total.

"I'm going to help you with your shipment today," explained Meadows. "We have three strangers in town, armed to the teeth." The lawman held his right hand on his six-shooter as he and the guards entered the bank with the money bags.

The guards opened the sacks and placed the money in the vault. The bank manager along with the guards counted the cash, $13,000 in all, and signed the appropriate paperwork. The guards thanked the marshal for his assistance, walked out the front doors, and climbed back on the top of the stagecoach. The driver let out a yell and his horses pulled the coach out of town, dust swirling behind them.

Deputy Sanders sat across the street in a small café to watch the activities at the bank, as two men appeared when the guards left the bank. They wore long dusters and neckerchiefs covering their faces presumably to keep out the blowing dust. He couldn't get a good look at their faces from his position across the street. They sat on a long bench, outside the front of the bank as if waiting for something or somebody. The marshal remained inside the bank.

Soon another cowboy rode to the front of the bank. Slowly getting off his black steed, the rider reached into his saddle bag and rummaged through it. Pulling a Sharps rifle from its scabbard, he loaded bullets into his lever-action weapon. The man slowly walked up the steps of the bank to its large front doors. His silver spurs and straps glowed in the sunlight.

The stranger slowly turned, and Sanders caught a good look at his face. He tried to swallow the lump in his throat, Oh my God; it's Mack and his boys. They're going to rob the bank.

Mack turned towards the two men sitting on the bench and said, "Let's do it." The two men got up; each grabbing their weapons and all three entered the bank.

Once inside, Mack yelled out. "Hands up, this here's a robbery!"

Marshal Meadows, still in the bank manager's office, heard the robber's orders. He whispered for the manager to be still. "We can't let them know I'm here.

The lawman pulled out his .41 caliber Colt Lightning and watched from his vantage point. He witnessed the robbers order a clerk to get the money from the safe. Mack, obviously the leader, held his weapon on the clerk's head and led him to another room, where the safe was located.

Meanwhile, Sanders had come across the street from the café to the bank's front windows. Mack's companions crouched with their handguns drawn, watching some of the bank employees and a few customers. Sanders, hands shaking, moved to a position behind a stack of logs near the corner of the building, and aimed his model 1883 Colt shotgun at the bank door.

Mack extracted several bundles of cash, placing each in a bag he had pulled from under his coat. "Stay in the room," he commanded the shaken clerk, and slowly backed out of the room. As he exposed himself to the others in the front lobby, the marshal shouted. "You're covered boys, drop your weapons."

Hearing this, Mack whirled around, his Colt revolver outstretched in his right hand. His partners turned in the direction of Meadows' voice. The marshal, hid behind the bank president's desk, had a clear shot at the robbers.

"I'll shoot everyone in here if you try to stop us." Mack yelled back, his spurs jingling as he kept moving slowly towards his two compadres.

Squared-jawed Henry Burrow, nervously blinked as sweat dripped down his forehead. "Let's get out of here," he screamed, and slowly backed towards the front doors, keeping his shaking handgun pointed at his victims.

Meadows held his position, but did not fire a shot at the robbers. Curt Johnson, the bank president, knelt next to the marshal, repeatedly mopping his brow with his handkerchief.

Mack grabbed a female customer's left arm. "You're coming with me!"---"What's you name honey?"

"Maggie Smith...please don't hurt me or anyone else!" Her hands shook in fear.

"Well, Maggie, that depends on how well everyone cooperates." He glared at his fellow robbers, threw a couple of money bags to his fellow hoodlums, and shouted. "Slowly move outside. We don't want to alarm anyone that the bank is being robbed."

"Crazy" Clark put his .44 Colt under his overcoat and clutched the money bag in his other hand. As he opened the front door, he was met with a hail of buckshot. The booming sound of the gunshot blast echoed down the street.

Clark fell to the sidewalk in front of the bank. "I'm hit, watch yourselves boys!"

He rolled over on his side and attempted to see who had shot him, the blowing dust temporarily obscured his vision.

Sanders crouched behind the log pile, reloaded his shotgun, and began squinting from the blowing sand and dust. His cover blew off his head, rolling down the street.

Citizens, apparently hearing the blast from the shotgun, came to the doors of their business, fully armed.

Inside the bank Meadows whispered, "Who the hell shot him?" He knew it was a desperate situation with several citizens' lives at risk, but felt he had to make his move. If they could get to the streets, with the dust storm for cover, they might all get away.

Rising from his position, the marshal aimed his .41 Colt Lightning and fired. A puff of smoke shot out of the barrel. His aim was straight and a slug ripped through Burrow's arm, making him spill his sack of cash. Blood sprayed from his half blown-off right arm as he hit the floor, screaming in agony.

Mack swirled around still holding his hostage in front of him for protection from any brave person who might fire at him. Dropping his money sack, he raised his pistol with his left hand, and fired it. But his aim was poor due to Maggie's struggle.

Outside the bank "Crazy" Clark realized where the shotgun blast had come from. He cocked the hammer of his

.44 and fired a shot at the nearby log pile. Splinters of wood flew everywhere, and piles of logs began to fall.

Sanders rose to his left knee and took aim at the bleeding bandit. He fired another round. Dark smoke and fire flew from his shotgun. But the blast missed its mark. Clark straightened his arm, and fired back. This time the bullet ripped through the lawman's chest, knocking him backwards onto several pieces of broken wood. The shot had gone right through him. Mortally wounded, blood ran profusely, soaking in the blowing dust that began to cover his motionless corpse.

Clark struggled to a standing position and fired another blast from his revolver to make sure the deputy was dead. His duster flapped in the swirling winds.

Inside the bank, Mack lost his grip on his female hostage. He attempted to grab the money bag while trying to fire a shot from his Sharps rifle, hanging on his shoulder. Maggie ran for cover behind a bank clerk's desk.

The marshal yelled, "Surrender or be killed!" As he attempted to get up to peek over the top of the desk, Burrow's pistol blasted, the slug just missed him. He fell backwards, breathing hard. That was a close one.

Mack yelled to Burrow, "Take the money bag and let's get to our horses." Turning he ran out the large front doors of the bank. The winds hit violently and momentarily stopped him in his tracks. In his attempt to cover his eyes with his left arm, he dangled the money bag. Burrow backed out of the bank firing wildly from his pistol.

As Burrow went out the front door, the marshal pointed his trusty handgun and fired, hitting him in his belly. Burrow's limp body fell backwards to the bank steps. His prone body lay motionlessly.

Hearing that gunshot from inside the bank, Mack turned around and fired a couple more shots into the bank, hitting a bank patron in his knee. "Let's get to our mounts and get the hell out of here."

Mack leaped on his horse as Burrow slowly lumbered to his mount, bleeding heavily from his wound.

A local grocery merchant, standing at an alley nearby, pulled his Smith & Wesson Model .38. Trying desperately to steady his aim in the strong wind, he fired his weapon, striking Burrow in his left shoulder. Burrow broke his grip on his money sack and reeled his horse around to see who had shot him.

Meadows ran to the front of the banks doors, slightly pushing opened one side. He took careful aim and fired his Colt. The bullet stuck Burrow's neck. Blood sprayed in the wind, mixing with the sand and dust. The wounded bandit fell to the ground.

Mack turned his horse around and saw his buddy was a goner. He spurred his horse and galloped off into a cloud of dust.

Meadows fired a blast from his weapon, striking Mack in his back.

Mack reeled his mount to an abrupt stop. Turning his horse, he strained to see through the whirling dusk. When he caught sight of the marshal, Mack nodded his head. Grinning slightly, he reined his mount and galloped away, vanishing down the dusty road, out of town.

By mid-afternoon the winds ceased, and locals looked at the carnage of dead and wounded citizens. Deputy Milt Sanders died, leaving a wife and four small children. Bank robbers Gerald Clark and Henry Burrow were also dead; both of their money bags retrieved by bank officials. The customer with the wounded knee, lost his life due to loss of blood. It was indeed a bloody day in Caldwell.

A posse searched for the escaped leader of the bandits but no trace of him was ever found. The legend and mystery of his fate is still a topic of discussion today. Some believe he lived and traveled back to his homestead, living as a cattle baron until his death in the 1920s. Others felt he died from his wounds, his remains consumed by animals. Some could care less.

What of the money he stole? Some heard the amount stolen was an estimated $3,500. Accounts of the bank officials and newspaper reports differed to the actual amount taken.

Whatever it was, "Shorty" Mack's legend grows with each passing generation and shall never be forgotten!

THE MAN WITH TWO GRAVES

by

Dixie Maxwell

The creeping decline of old age filled James with a sense of urgency. His children didn't know the secret that burdened his conscience, and he considered leaving it that way, but he didn't. This is the story he wrote to his children:

I was a young man when the judge said, "A jury of your peers has found you guilty. I hereby sentence you to three years in prison."

Three years. The gavel came down, and it didn't escape my notice that my peers chose not to look me in the eye as they filed out of the room. In a place charged with meting out justice, there was plenty of injustice in the courtroom that day. All of it piled on me. I directed my attention to my worthless lawyer. "Do something. Get me out of here. My family needs me." All I got was a shrug as he shuffled his papers. He didn't make even the slightest effort to apologize for his lousy effort on my behalf. A deputy with a gun holstered on his belt put his hand on my shoulder and I instantly regretted every poor choice and lie I ever told.

As we left the courthouse, I made one last plea to the deputy. "Is there any chance I can get a new trial or a new jury?"

"Nope. Tough luck, kid. I can't do anything about your situation."

Men with vacant eyes lined the sidewalks. Jobs were scarce in the summer of 1929, and a man's dignity was just as scarce. The deputy walked me over to the train depot and handed me off to another deputy waiting to board with a convict. People stared and shrank back when they saw the black and white stripes of our prisoner clothing. I didn't blame them. Prisoners were a bad lot, no doubt about it. I was glad my mother would never see how I shamed our family.

"Last chance to use the facilities, gentlemen. It's now or two hours from now."

I opted for now in the hopes of a possible escape. No luck. The zebra suit worked against me, and there was no way to blend into the crowd. When we returned to our train car, the deputy cuffed my right hand to my seatmate's left hand, and then walked away. I looked down at our hands. Mine was young and strong with hardly a blemish except for a fading bruise on my knuckles, but his was a hand that had seen plenty of use and abuse. Either he was a hard worker, or a rounder given to fist fights on a regular basis. I suspected he was both. He spoke first.

"What's your name, kid?"

"James Lewis. What's yours?"

He looked at me and a slow smile twisted the outer corners of his mouth. "James Lewis, huh? Now that's a name I can work with. What're you in for, and how long?"

"Attempted robbery, and assault. I tried to steal a loaf of bread, but the shopkeeper tripped me on the way out, and I fell. I sprang up and socked him in the jaw, but he was tougher than I expected, and wrestled me to the floor. "I can pay," I grunted, but he didn't believe me, and asked to see my money. I didn't have any money, and the jury didn't have any mercy. I got a three-year sentence. You didn't tell me your name."

"My name is Jay Louis, and today is your lucky day. Listen closely. I think you'll like what I have to say."

As a captive audience, I didn't have anything else to do, so I listened. Jay Louis was a repeat offender, and his latest sentence was a ten-year term. A rookie inmate like me was lucky to get the lay of the land from the likes of him. That's what I thought until I heard his proposition.

"The way I see it, kid, the similarity in our names is the perfect set-up for an identity switch. When we check in, I'll tell them your name, and you'll tell them mine."

Either he was off his rocker or thought I was off mine. I gave him a side glance to make sure he wasn't kidding me. He wasn't.

"You want me to trade my three-year sentence for your ten? No thanks."

"Hear me out. True, a switch seems to work more in my favor than yours, but be patient and I'll explain. I've been in and out of jail for most of my life. Another ten years will be the end of me, but three years will give me time to rest, and get some decent meals under my belt. The country is in a mess now, but three years from now it could be on the road back to normal."

"Wait a minute . . ."

He jerked my wrist. "You won't serve ten years, because you're going to escape. I've never been in McAlester Prison, but rumor has it that men escape from Big Mac on a regular basis. Get a job in the shoe plant, the tailor shop, or the roads crew, and you'll be out and gone before anyone has time to miss you."

Escape? I couldn't manage to steal a simple loaf of bread, and he thought I could figure out how to get out of a place ringed with razor wire and guarded by men with guns? The idea horrified me.

"You're a nice kid. You should have the life you were meant to live. As long as no one comes to visit either of us, the switch will work."

"All I have is my little sister. She lives with our grandma, and they barely have money for food. I feel bad about the worry I've piled on their heads, but if I'm lucky they'll never know where I am."

"Good. Any friend I ever had is long gone by now, and my family gave up on me years ago. Tell you what . . . if we get close to the three-year mark, and you haven't managed to get free of this place, we'll call attention to the in-take error, and you'll be released."

I looked at the countryside slipping past the window, and then at my rundown shoes. They were my only personal possession, and my future looked as bleak as they did. I doubted they'd last another three years. I'd never gambled money, because I didn't have any, but the way my luck was going I figured the odds were with my shoes when it came to lasting. The switch scheme was crazy, but I was running low on hope and it was worth considering. I ran it through my mind over and over, and before long the future I thought I might never see seemed possible again. Jay Louis was a total stranger, and a convict to boot, but for reasons I can't explain, I trusted him. I agreed to the switch as we pulled into the station.

"Okay. We'll do it your way."

Jay Louis nodded and that was that.

Later that first night as I lay in my hard, narrow bunk, the cries and moans of helpless, hopeless men filled the darkness and I was afraid. Jay was right . . . I didn't belong in that place. I prayed all night for divine intervention. The next morning my first thought was 'I gotta get out of here'.

Jay Louis was housed in another area of the prison, and I never saw him again. Getting into prison was the easy part. It was the getting out that took some imagination. I kept thinking of the ten years, or three if Jay kept his word, and saw my future slipping away as surely as rain off the roof. I hadn't lived long enough to make many plans, but none of even the most basic included prison. I didn't feel like I deserved prison even if my peers thought otherwise, so I talked myself into thinking an escape was the right thing to do. It wasn't, but being surrounded day and night by ruthless men hardened by bad luck and bad choices was a powerful motivator. My first two escape attempts were failures, but I learned from my mistakes, and finally managed to get free on my third.

The details of my escape aren't important, but I credit Jay for stirring up the courage I needed to keep trying. I never regretted my escape. Especially later. I was on my way through Missouri when I met your mother. She was a looker for sure, but it was her sweetness and generous spirit that sealed the deal for me. The day we married was the best day of my life . . . until our children were born.

~

James and Dorothy had a long run, but on a cold December day decades after their marriage, James was laid to rest. Dorothy and their children stood at his grave, their grief as raw as the frigid wind that stung their faces. Jay, Mary, and Jesse hugged their mother as she stood rigid and silent next to a mound of bare earth. Their eyes went to their father's name on the double headstone. The date of his death would be added later, but seeing his name on that cold hard stone had a finality about it that brought tears to their eyes.

"I must go home now, to prepare for tomorrow," Dorothy said.

"What happens tomorrow?"

"It was your father's wish that when this day came I would take you to his other grave, and give you letters that he wrote to each of you before he died. We must leave early.

"What other grave, where will we go, what are these letters, and why can't we have them now?"

Dorothy raised her hand. Weary from grief and dreading the day ahead of her, she didn't have the energy or the will to answer their questions.

"Your father was a good man. He took care of our family, served faithfully in our church, and took an active interest in the community, but there was more to his life than you know. All of your questions will be answered tomorrow. Go home and rest. We have a long day head of us. We'll leave at 6:00 a.m."

Their nine-hour road trip took them to McAlester, Oklahoma, where the prison dominated the skyline. They hardly noticed the cemetery near the prison walls until Dorothy directed Jay to drive to the gate. Peckerwood Hill Cemetery was unlike any other cemetery they had ever seen. All the markers were flat white stones that hugged the earth in narrow rows with no ornamentation or plantings to break up the field.

A security guard allowed them to enter, and Dorothy reached for Mary's hand as she struck out across the grounds. "They call this the orphan's or pauper's cemetery. Prisoners who have no family to claim their remains are buried here. Two more rows."

Dorothy stopped, and they looked down at a white stone marker with their father's name on it. JAMES J. LEWIS, 1909-1929.

"What is this? What does it mean?"

Dorothy handed each of them a letter from her purse and watched as they tore into them and began reading.

Jay looked from his letter to the marker. "So Jay Louis is the one buried here?"

"Yes, and you can see from the date that he wasn't here even a year before he died. Your father and I, and you too, owe this man a debt of gratitude. Dad and I have been here several times through the years to pay our respects."

"Do you know how he died?"

"Yes. A group of men jumped a guard in the yard, and Jay tried to help him. Jay was stabbed and died, but the guard lived."

"He saved our father's life, too, didn't he?"

"Probably, maybe. The switch idea was risky, but your father was smart enough and desperate enough to give it a try and it paid off for him. Jay Louis didn't live to see his part of the plan through, but in a way he got out of jail earlier than he expected. When we heard he went out a hero, we were happy for him."

Jesse stooped to run his hand over the weathered stone. "It's hard to see Dad's name in this place. Do you know how he escaped?"

"He told me the whole story before he proposed. We agreed to never speak of it again. He didn't want the particulars to become exaggerated or glorified in any way. All I will tell you is that no one was injured during his escape, and no one ever came looking for him."

"So, you won't tell us?"

"No. I want you to remember your father as a good dad, and not think of him as a jailbird. He tried to steal the bread because his baby sister was hungry and cried herself to sleep every night. It wasn't the right thing to do, but he had good intentions."

"Do you know what happened to his sister and grandmother?" Mary whispered.

"As soon as your father got a few dollars together, he mailed them to his grandmother and continued to send what he could until Mary reached adulthood. She had a good life, and died several years ago. No husband or children, in case you're curious about possible cousins.

Today is about your father, and I want you to remember all the big and little things he did through the years to give you good, rich lives. On the way over here, I thought of how he cheered at your ball games, built a playhouse in the backyard, and taught you to swim in the creek. In my opinion, things in the past should stay there, but your father thought it was important to set the record straight."

Jay put his arm around his mother's thin shoulders. "We'll never forget any of those things, Mom. We all loved him very much, and he's always been our hero. What we

[119]

learned today won't change that. In fact, now we know he was more heroic than any of us ever imagined. Thanks for bringing us here today. Now I know how I came to get my name."

Dorothy wiped the tears from her face. "I thought we should name you James after your dad, but he said if not for Jay he might never have lived to be a dad. When you were little, I called you J-Jay. That was my way of calling you both names."

Jay smiled. "I remember that."

Dorothy sighed. "Who knew an ordinary family could have so many secrets. I hope you'll pay special attention to the last few lines of your father's letter. He wanted you to know his story, and hoped it wouldn't change how you feel about him. But most of all, he wanted you to know how much he loved each of you. He was a good man."

They looked down at their letters.

Their father's handwriting suffered toward the end, but they had no trouble reading his final words:

If you're reading this letter, I'm gone from this world. I love you very much, and hope you won't judge your old man too harshly for his misstep in the past. Even after all these years, I'm ashamed of my behavior and hope you will keep my revelations within our family. "All things work together for good" and I'm forever thankful for the jailbird switch that brought me to your mother, and to our family.

It has been an honor and pleasure to be your father, to watch you grow and mature into outstanding adults. I give your mother plenty of credit for your success, but I like to think you got some of your fierce loyalty and determination from me.

Don't be afraid to take chances. You are capable of more than you can imagine. Life sometimes gets in the way of living, but if you try your best, good things will come. If you ever find yourself in an impossible situation, maybe the information in this letter will give you the courage you need to forgive someone, trust someone, or step out in faith when the odds seem stacked against you.

Love each other and take care of your mother.

Don't let the other grave marker trouble you . . . we all die eventually and get buried . . . some of us twice.

Love, Dad

Poetry and Essays

Discarded Heroes of World War II
An Essay by
Robert Cooper

Why have the history books ignored the contributions of some people? Do what the history books contain really reflect what happened, or is it only what certain individuals want us to believe transpired?

These questions came to light several decades ago during my association with Max, (not his real name). We were business colleagues back in the 70's. One day over lunch, he told me that he had been in the "Big War" (World War II). He said he had been a colonel in the Polish Army, but he did not fight the Germans on the battlefields of Europe. Instead, he traveled back and forth between England and Poland. Sounds a lot like a spy, doesn't it! One of the stories he told me was how the Allies had broken Germany's cipher code and that they knew a considerable amount about what the Germans were planning well in advance of them actually executing those plans. Even as late as 1973, that information was not common knowledge. His stories intrigued me, but I will admit to being somewhat skeptical as to whether they were true or just fell in the realm of fiction. I decided to do some research into what he had told me. What he had said concerning the cipher code was true. For me that made the rest of his stories very plausible. It also made him one of those unsung heroes that we never hear about.

Max's story deserved to be told. I tried to persuade him to write his memoirs and even offered to help, but he did not want any part of it. His reluctance made me realize that there was something in his past that he did not want to share with others, so I honored his wishes and dropped the subject.

Decades later when I found out, he had passed away, I decide to write his story. Utilizing what he had told me as a starting point, I began my research. I was shocked to learn what I knew about World War II was like a huge block of Swiss cheese with plenty of gaping holes in it. My research revealed four incredible facts that were never taught in school.

The first one dealt with the whole story surrounding Germany's Top Secret Enigma Cipher Code Project. It seems that the French were the first to get their hands on a copy of the project's user manual. It was photographed back in 1928 by one of France's spies. The French tried to use the manual to build a working model of the machine and to break the code. They failed. The French then turned it over to the English. They too failed. The English then turned it over to Poland's Intelligence Group. In 1932, three Polish mathematicians and cipher experts did what no one else could do. They not only built a working model of the machine, they also broke the code. In 1938, just prior to the outbreak of the war, Poland shared what they had learned with the French and English. Bletchley Park would probably have been nothing more than a radio station for the Allies and not the major decoding center as it is known for without these men.

The second thing I discovered concerns who was actually involved in the war, and on whose side, they fought. The following countries had troops fighting on the Allied side, Belgium, Brazil, Czechoslovakia, Denmark, Estonia, Latvia, Lithuania, Netherlands, New Zealand, Norway, Poland, South Africa and Yugoslavia. The countries that joined the Axis Powers were Bulgaria, Croatia, Hungary, Iraq, Romania, Slovakia, Thailand and Vichy France. This was a total shock to me. Simply because I was under the assumption that the only combatants in the war were from Australia, Canada, China, France, Greece, India, United Kingdom, United States, Russia, Germany, Italy and Japan.

The third item dealt with what Poland's army did during the war. Apparently, after Poland fell in 1939, units of the Army made their way to France and fought alongside the French and English against the Germans. They first fought to save France from falling into German hands. As we know, France fell in 1940. After that, these same Polish units fought with distinction alongside the other Allied countries involved in the war until its end in 1945.

Units of the Polish Army that did not flee Poland 1939 formed resistance groups. These groups fought the Germans using kidnapping, assassination and sabotage methods. When the Russians forced the Germans out of Poland and took their place as conquerors, these same groups continued their struggle to remove the Russian invaders from their homeland. These groups were so successful in their endeavor against both enemies that the Germans and then the Russians took out their frustrations on the populous. They executed dozens or even hundreds of innocent civilians every time the underground pulled off a successful mission. Eventually their struggle against the Russians and the communist government that they had set up began to take its toll on these brave men and women, and in the end, the survivors simply faded away.

The final piece of information that I uncovered concerned the real heroes of the war. It seems that while Hitler was planning to take over the world, the Polish Intelligence Agency known as The Sixth Bureau was busy building up a spy network throughout Europe. When the war broke out, France and England had nothing remotely capable of competing with Poland's organization. In the second half of 1940, the Brits took over The Sixth Bureau's assets and placed them under their own agency, which was called SOE. If it had not been for the brave men and women who originally worked under the umbrella of the Sixth Bureau, who knows how the war might have ended.

Even though this article focuses on the people of Poland, this in no way diminishes the contributions and accomplishments of those from other nations that were involved in that terrible conflict.

In my book, "Never Let the Meat Touch the Metal", I relate the real heroes are not just the ones who sit on their ivory thrones in the history books, but the ones history has deliberately ignored and taken for granted. The book is labeled historical fiction and is about one man's suspense filled journey through a war, which never should have been, and how he unintentionally uncovers the real secrets behind it.

Sources for this article can be found on Wikipedia and are entitled:

Polish Contributions to World War Two

Polish Resistance Movement in World War Two

PC Bruno - (it is about the breaking of the German cipher code)

Durkirk Evacuation

Breaking Germany's Enigma Code by Andrew Lycett

THE WEEDS AMONG US
An essay by
Barbara Lockett

The spring weeds in my yard grow two feet high before there is any sign of grass. This year the cold, wet weather interfered with my yearly attack on the weeds. Constant, heavy rains, beyond the ones I remember from past seasons, kept me inside. As a result, the tall henbit sheltered the ground-hugging weeds. At age six I loved the pretty purple flowerets on their stems. Another prime example is sheep shower spread out in large patches over the ground. We used to nibble it as children. Remember?

I say right now, "I hate weeds with the same passion a teen-age kid hates the appearance of an ugly outlaw zit on his otherwise clear-skinned face." I have been dealing with weeds for 15 or 20 years. During that time, the weeds have multiplied more and more each year, to a degree, I have almost given up and let them take over my yard. In trying to reign death on the ever-spreading patches of low-growth weeds, by poisoning or pulling them out, I discovered the similarity between weeds and people. I know both intimately, up close and personal.

Some kinds of people have much in common with weeds. They imitate legitimate plant growth the way sheep shower imitates white clover. Yes, the white clover with which we used to weave fanciful chains. Connecting the stems into chains and wearing those garlands around our necks were a graceful part of wonderful warm summer evenings.

That said, there are people who suck up to those honest and open souls among us. They pretend to be like us and may seem to be good company. Then, they become less sincere and begin taking advantage of their targets—us. They show up and say, "I don't have a car. Will you take me to the Wall Mart?" or, "I'm out of meat. Let me go with you to the market." Then you wait while your fellow shopper goes up and down every aisle of the store loading up sacks of groceries which you have to help carry to your car. Weed people continue their excuses to the point of, "I forgot my billfold. Lend me $20. I'll pay you right back." Then like book borrowers, you never see the book, or the $20, again.

They may bring their chums over for coffee or a meal. Their friends, like the weeds, cling on to act the same way they do. "Come on, guys. I got a great place for you." Yes, weeds talk to each other. Dig down into the weedy lawn. You will see weeds entwining their stems into the blade joints of grass where those stems will multiply and remain. They may succeed in choking out all plant growth.

Now observe. Pull out the weed and look at its root. Many varieties have roots than end in fuzzy little rootlets, soft little spheres branching out, which fasten into the ground coming to new life over and over. The fully grown weed tends to break off when you pull it out. Because you break the stem away from the little fuzz ball, it will just grow another weed. You have to dig it out. See them in human form. Butter wouldn't melt in their mouths. They are insidious, turning up here and there, calling when you are in a hurry. They can be surly and sarcastic. These include telephone sales callers and those who call for charitable donations. They attempt to shame you, if you cannot give to their cause. It is best to be polite and thank them for the opportunity, but no thanks. Then cut them off and hang up. Don't explain. It just encourages them.

Some weeds have long, stickery roots. It is best to pull them out after a ground softening rain. Don't wait and let the clay soil harden. It is hard work digging at them with even a sharp pointed tool. If you can, apply weed killer over and over to give your grass space to grow when it begins its season in May. If you haven't the means, or the time, you are left to eliminate the weeds, hands on. You can do either of two things. Spend the summer mowing weeds or dig and pull them out with your own hands. I truly hate both ways.

But about weed people. Cut them out of your life. Better to see them coming before they get to you. Do not let them get close enough to begin choking off your freedom.

I once knew a girl whose surname was Leach. She certainly lived up to her name. She would meet me on the church steps and not let go until I had taken her home after the service. Then she would repeat her actions the next time. This happened in my inexperienced youth, when I had no real knowledge of weeds in the ground, or of people. I had to learn to be unavailable. At last, I was relieved of the Leach by a job move to another town. Thank God.

To avoid the weeds among us, you must simply cut off attachments with them! If not, beware. You have been warned.

A Christmas Prayer
by
Michelle Walker

Dear God,

I'm here to say a special prayer of something really on my heart. I ask that you listen closely, because the message tears me apart.

As I look around this Christmas and I see the jubilee, Christmas rush and happy faces, packages adorning Christmas trees,

I can't help but think of others who aren't in this scene I see. Those of homeless, wrecked lives, children without a family.

I watch the merry shoppers, laced with presents to the brim, then I think about the dear child who needs shoes and a coat to keep warm.

Dear God,

What will happen to him?
A child born in a manger has become so commercialized, that we hardly seem to remember that this Child saved our lives.

You see God,

I want so much this Christmas, to enjoy all that I have.
My friends, a home, a family and a heaven up ahead.
So help me reach my hand today, to put a smile upon each face,

And remind those all around me, it was Jesus' saving grace.

Summers When I Was Young
By
Carol Snow

Saturday afternoons my friends and I
walked to town for dime movies
where Gene Autry and the Durango Kid
thwarted bad guys' schemes.

Weekdays we roamed the country
behind my grandmother's house
wading streams, collecting snails,
horny toads and turtles.

Evenings we jumped rope
or sat on the warm sidewalk playing jacks
while adults talked on the porch--
joking, exchanging news, hopes, dreams.

After dark grandparents told stories—
coming to Oklahoma in covered wagons,
panther screams at night, outlaw gangs,
rowdy oil-boom towns.

Their childhood seemed so strange
so exotic, so different from mine
as strange as these sweet memories
must seem to my own grandchildren.

A Desert Night

by

Rae Neal

If there were no voices to speak,
If there were no words to express,
If there were no eyes to perceive,
The silence would remain silent,
The stillness would underwhelm.
No creature's heart could grasp
The significance of a desert night
Lit by the heavens natural light.

Starlight canopies the nighttime sky.
The air is fresh and nippy.
Fire pit smoke curls out over the desert
And spreads the sweet aroma of burning pinon.
A rabbit darts quietly around the cacti.
An outline of mountains rises in the distance,
Marks the desert floor's edge,
Lends measure to perceptiveness.

Silence surrounds and suspends loudly,
Summons a whisper of recognition,
A verbal contemplation of design,
An acknowledgement of scenic beauty.
Without human expression of the glory,
Effusiveness of descriptive speech,

A heralding of creation's uniqueness,

What is left to appreciate the created?

Must design then remain useless?
Must beauty be left emptied of marvel?
Mustn't creation exist for an observer?

A desert night has ability to calm
As when morning arises to a new day;
To appease as water satisfies thirst;
To refresh as sleep replenishes a body.

Surely there must be a mind
Honed by its spirit to relate,
An ability to comprehend,
To touch surroundings with thought,
To transfer musings to the tongue
And deliver through its heart filter
The significance of its visual plane.
A nighttime desert's attributes
Broadcasted and given tribute
Lends credence to its existence
And gives cause for its design.

Take me to the desert of the night
Where the sky sparkles above,
Hangs low overhead yet alludes,
Its roof blended with sanded floor;
Where a fire pit glows red and orange;
Where scents of burning pine fill my senses
And I will declare the glory to all who hear:

Creation is the work of genius, not man.

[136]

Design is wrought by intelligence—
A mind that far exceeds a rabbit's scamper,
A heart that knows true beauty
And created a desert night.

The Happy Poet's Lament

by

Beverly Strader

I won't rant.
Don't ask me.
Life is good.
I'm happy.
I've no need to rant and rave.

Kids all grown
And paid for.
Pets all gone.
Don't want more.
Now's the time to celebrate.

So slam on
Without me.
Rant and rave.
That's not me.
Think I'll head out to the lake.
Right after the nap I'm gonna take.

Modern Fiction

Being Thelma and Louise
by
Nikki Hanna

Mom was seventy-five and I fifty-four when we became *Thelma and Louise.* I'd say, "Get in the car, Thelma." Her eyes would light up like a child discovering a spotted puppy. Always up for an adventure, she grabbed her purse and cane and shuffled to the garage at an amazing pace given her bad knees.

Before Dad died, he often surprised Mom with spontaneous escapades. When he said, "Get in the car, Mom," she was ready. They set off for destinations to which she was not privy until they got there. I suspect my invitations reminded her of those impromptu adventures, and that she delighted in the feelings our trips resurrected.

Mom never saw the *Thelma and Louise* movie, so she wasn't sure what to think when I assigned us that label. She seemed up for it, though. There was no protest when I announced that I got to be Louise, the character who shot somebody—not that Mom would have wanted that role anyway. An Iowa farm woman immersed in heartland conformity, she was not inclined to aspire to criminal activity.

After Dad died, I brought her from rural Iowa to Tulsa, Oklahoma, for long visits to distract from the grief that threatened to overwhelm her. She was in a vulnerable state. In addition to the loss of Dad, declining physical abilities were taking hold. The responsibility of caring for her weighed on me. I worried she would fall. She had a small dog who was on his last leg. He accompanied her on those visits. I was concerned he would die on my watch and generate even more grief. I also agonized over the prospect that Mom would trip over him, fall on him, hurt herself, and kill the dog.

Since I worked, Mom sat alone all day surveilling neighborhood activity through a window as she occupied herself with jigsaw puzzles, word games, and crochet. Out of her element in my downtown Tulsa townhouse, she expressed considerable curiosity about the destinations of passing cars. In her rural environment, she could predict where neighbors' were headed by the direction they were going, the day of the week, and the time of day. The anonymity of my neighbors and my lack of interest in their business baffled her.

Feeling guilty about leaving her alone all day, I planned adventures for the evenings. We patronized our favorite restaurants. The extensive menus and generous portions disturbed her. She would say, "I'll just eat off your plate," which irritated me. Her extreme frugality prompted her to stuff table items and condiments into her purse and to carry plastic bags in which to store table scraps and a knife with which to cut them up.

After dinner, we hit craft stores and specialty shops. I held her hand from the car to shopping carts, carefully navigating curbs, sidewalk flaws, and door jams. The tender nature of this action comforted me. Her hands were soft, her fingers long and slender, her grasp gentle but sure. We fit together with a naturalness possible only through common ancestry. I have her hands. My daughter does as well. I look at my granddaughter's tiny hands and wonder . . .

We developed an easy banter, and she took on the mission of getting the better of me. This drew out the smart aleck in me, which she pretended to find disgusting but secretly enjoyed. The upward curl of her lips and the sparkle in her eyes betrayed her.

Detailers left the moonroof cover open on my car. I pushed every button in that vehicle trying to close it, creating a host of other problems. This included interior lights permanently lit, which had me driving around town looking like an all-night casino. I complained about the predicament to Mom as we took off on a road trip. She reached up, slid the moonroof cover shut, and sat there smiling like a Cheshire cat who had left a fur ball on my spot on the sofa. I decided to take advantage of her mechanical aptitude. I asked, "Why don't you shut off the interior lights, smart ass?" And she did.

Although we were girlfriends, she didn't abandon her maternal role completely. I often read into the night, which in her mind was wrong. She showed up in my bedroom doorway late one night in a nightgown with a floral pattern representative of wallpaper. Wild-eyed and wobbly, everything about her seemed askew. Her hair resembled a cat toy caught in a fishing lure. Waving her cane, she was a scary sight.

"You're going to go blind," she scolded in a raspy voice.

A patronizing lecture ensued against which I held my position, "You are not the boss of me."

She eventually shuffled back to bed, mumbling something about a home for the blind and debtors' prison. As my heart rate returned to normal, I resumed reading.

Such a conniption fit was rare. Mom was generally meek and mild mannered. On our road trips, it was not uncommon for me to be stopped by the highway patrol. Having spent considerable time on patrol with sheriff's deputies in the past, I viewed any opportunity to interact with law enforcement as an adventure extraordinaire. In contrast, Mom was traumatized the second the blue and red lights started flashing. She never did acclimate to the experience, and it did not comfort her that we never got a ticket.

That was because Mom was just the sidekick I needed to get out of one. I had developed a nifty, failsafe routine to do so. Here's how it worked:

Mom looked like Mrs. Santa Claus—short, round, white hair, and old-fashioned glasses. She sported a silver helmet-head hairdo and calico print dresses. A purse always hung from her arm àla Queen Elizabeth's style.

When pulled over, I rolled down the window, pointed to her, and told the patrolman, "She made me do it."

When he leaned down to take a look, he discovered Mom in the passenger seat, frozen with fear. Her lack of eye contact was reminiscent of a dog who had peed on the living room rug. The only movement was from her hands in her lap, wringing a handkerchief.

After allowing the patrolman time to take that in, I asked, "Would you take her to jail?"

If that didn't get a laugh, I whispered, "You know, she kidnapped me."

When additional drama was required, I applied my *coup d'état* and told him, "We are *Thelma and Louise*, and *she* is the one who shot somebody."

An Oklahoma patrolman called my bluff when I asked him to take Mom to jail. In a strong southern accent, he said, "I'd do that, ma'am, but I *would* have to tase her first." That produced an unpleasant visual in my mind, and I decided to skip the kidnapping routine and allow him the last word.

"Your passenger looks suspicious—a threat to any community," he said. "Git on down the road to Missouri and don't make any stops along the way."

We didn't get a ticket.

I took Mom everywhere, even out with my single friends. The guys asked her out on dates, and I threatened to shoot them. Married all her life, she was perplexed by my single lifestyle. Terrorizing her over my exploits became a temptation too enticing to resist.

Dressed in leather pants for a date, I asked her, "Am I sexy yet?"

I followed up with, "I wear leather on dates so I smell like a new truck."

Borrowing one of Dad's lines, she said, "You are one watt short of a nightlight."

In spite of that protestation, she must have thought I looked smart, because she took my picture. As I was leaving with my date, she said, "Don't call me if you get thrown in jail."

This was a familiar threat I had heard often during my teenage years. It was confounding to my date, though. His plans for the evening did not include getting arrested.

Thelma and I haunted a casino primarily for the buffet—or so we said. In Mom's mind, gambling was a sin. She made me promise not to reveal her vice to church friends in Iowa.

We were not sophisticated gamblers. The first time we hit the casino, we carried baggies of coins from my change jar. I had no idea slot machines had gone coinless years ago. And I was shocked and disappointed to discover the levers had been replaced with buttons. Yes, buttons. A casino security officer observed us old ladies trying to locate an opening for coins in a penny slot machine. He oriented us on the modern nuances of gambling. In return, we were rude and inconsiderate.

"Shoot. I wanted to pull the handles," Mom complained to him while frantically pounding buttons and staring transfixed at spinning cherries.

"Me, too. This is a bummer," I said, as I hammered away on my own buttons.

In ten minutes our money was gone, and we ambled over to the buffet.

I took Mom on trips. She was a novice traveler, having rarely been out of Iowa, or even her own community. We ventured all the way to Hawaii, where she worried about being a burden to me.

"If I get sick, just throw me in the ocean," she said.

"I don't think my brothers would appreciate it if I took their mother on vacation and fed her to the sharks. I'll put you in a paraglider, though."

"I don't know what that is, but the idea sounds like something your dad would come up with."

I suspected she had that thought often. Although my physical characteristics mimicked Mom's, my way of being in the world had Dad written all over it.

Soon after arriving in Hawaii, we sat at a sidewalk cafe sipping pineapple drinks with umbrellas in them. Mom suddenly froze and took on an expression of grave concern.

"Mom, what's wrong?"

Through squinted eyes and with furrowed brow, she looked both ways to make certain no one could hear her. Leaning over the table, she whispered, "All these people here are foreigners." The perplexed look on her face when I explained that, in Hawaii, *she* was the foreigner, reflected the depth of her naïveté.

Having rarely left Iowa, Mom had little sense of other people or places. When we visited Salt Lake City, she worried the mountains would slide in on us. In Dallas, the traffic had her in a state of awesome wonder. She expressed a burning desire to know where all those people were going. After spending years in a small trailer and apartment, she could not grasp why anyone would want to ramble around in such big houses. In wonderful places she said, "I don't know why anyone would want to live here." This observation came from a woman who lived a couple of miles from a pig farm in Iowa. When the wind blew in the right direction, the place smelled like . . .like . . .like a pig farm.

On a trip to California, I took her to Venice Beach, which was like going to an extreme *Rocky Horror Picture Show* party.

I explained common beach apparel, "She's not naked as a jaybird, Mom. She's wearing a thong bikini."

I clarified beach activities, "No, Mom, body piercing is not a magic act."

I suggested brazen adventures, "Mom, let's get a tattoo. This skull and crossbones looks interesting. It's about pirates. We love pirates."

I don't believe she had ever seen a tattoo. She had a way of puffing her cheeks when something appalled her. Staring at a conspicuous tattoo of a lightning bolt shooting out of a young man's butt crack, she puffed like a blowfish. In her

Christmas letter that year, she wrote, "There sure are a lot of weird people in California."

She squeezed my hand tight and grabbed my arm as a pack of roller skaters whizzed by, barely missing us, as we ambled along the beach sidewalk. The skates made a horrendous racket, and their music blared the sort of sounds we old gals considered obnoxious nonsense.

"What the hell was that?" she asked.

Shocked, I responded, "Mom, you swore."

She covered her mouth and lowered her head in shame—mock shame, I suspected. Our adventures had inspired in her a newfound level of spunk. Reinforcing her moxie, I assured her that Thelma would, no doubt, have sworn in such a circumstance. In the past, the only time I ever heard her swear was when she fell on my front porch. I was so taken aback by her language that I failed to ask if she was hurt. Instead, I said, "Mom, you swore!"

As her health deteriorated, our excursions became limited to trips around her senior housing apartment in Iowa. We were still *Thelma and Louise,* but the days of big adventures were behind us. Over the years, festering health crises gained momentum. She went into a nursing home at eighty-eight, where she was chastised by church ladies for swearing during card games and disciplined by staff for speeding in her wheelchair.

In the midst of a severe medical episode, she slipped off her wedding ring, handed it to me, and we cried. She rallied the next day, so I put it back on her finger after which I held on tight to that precious hand that nurtured me all my life. It was clear where she was headed.

She died a few months later. The times we shared were sweet. We were girlfriends—carousing, teasing, and giggling. We were tight. We were *Thelma and Louise*, although we never shot anybody. And we never got a ticket.

The Second Friday of the Month
by
Pamela Wetterman

Elizabeth Phillips, unable to sleep, counted the minutes crawling past on her digital alarm. As if caught in a time warp, with only a few hours of sleep, her dreams awakened her anxiety. Coiled in bed, ready to react at a moment's notice, her senses were in overload. Last month's experience ignited her. Dare she hope for another perfect evening?

Elizabeth warmed as her husband, Jack, grunted in his sleep and buried his head in his pillows. The depth of her love for him surprised her. No male had touched her more tenderly, protected her unconditionally, or strengthened her more than Jack.

Snuggling closer to her husband, Elizabeth massaged his muscular back.

"Good morning. Time to join the living for another day."

He rolled over and stretched. His blond hair, tossed in all directions, concealed his aqua blue eyes. Pushing his wayward hair off his forehead, he smiled and drew her into an extended kiss—taunting her with his tongue.

[153]

"How can one man be so lucky? You're dazzling this morning."

A smile touched her lips as she nestled into his warmth. "Got any extra time this morning?"

"Sorry. Not today. We're training a new guy. Can't be late."

His stomach released a deep roar. She glanced at the clock. Yep. Right on schedule—time for breakfast. Good thing he accepted microwave magic.

As a child she'd dreamed of becoming a famous gourmet chef. By the age of twenty-two, her contact with cooking school ended with Dessert 101—more specifically, Cherries Jubilee soaked in brandy. The failed dessert removed any possibility of being a featured chef, even at local fast-food chain. The high-priced culinary school removed her name from its records before the firemen put out the blaze.

Not all was lost. One of the firefighters turned out to be Jack Phillips. Six months later, they were married. Two benefits of his profession—his talent as a cook, and his work schedule. Not only did he prepare her dinners, but his twenty-four-hour days required him to sleep at the firehouse four times a week. She maintained their two bedroom condo, the credit cards, and her free time. Nice.

After handing a Jimmy Dean's sausage biscuit to Jack, she walked him to his vehicle. Moving close, she brushed her lips against his cheek. He returned her passion with his.

He placed the palm of his hand against her cheek and gazed into her eyes. "This'll be a long weekend. Have fun. I'll give you a call as time opens up." He hopped into his red Ford-F-150, backed out of the drive, and turned north on Enfield Lane.

The summer breeze kissed her skin. She'd have no time for girlfriends this weekend. It was the second Friday of the month. Time to finalize her plans.

Elizabeth strolled into her office and lowered her five-foot-ten inch frame into the deep, blue leather chair behind her mahogany desk. July crept by like sand filling an hourglass. She'd dreamt of this night since last month.

Even as a teen, she'd required variety, adventure, mystery. She'd bored easily. The Every Second Friday Club filled her with excitement. Her membership benefits offered the inspiration she desired. She loved Jack, but…

The ringtone startled her. Who calls at seven in the morning? Glancing at the caller ID, she frowned. Of course, it had to be her mother-in-law.

"Hey, June. Morning. What can I do for you today?"

"Beth, dear. Hope I didn't call too early. Wanted to see if you'd be available to come by tonight and keep the kids."

Elizabeth chewed on her bottom lip. Kids. How many forty-something women in their third marriage, kept having babies? Each of her husbands, born closer and closer to Jack's age. If this marriage failed, she might find number four at the high school.

Jack fumed whenever the topic of his mother entered their conversation. He barely acknowledged all the half brothers and sisters created by his mom. She wouldn't face her age. God forbid she's called Granny.

These last two kids, both girls, were ten and twelve, and spoiled rotten. Most sitters refused to care for the kids a second time. No amount of money enticed them.

"Gee. Wish I could help you out, but my plans are set. Sorry."

"Well, can't you change them, just for tonight? Besides, Jack's working at the firehouse, overnight, right?"

How could one woman be so self-centered? It's amazing that Jack grew up without major personality issues.

"We're not available. Sorry, our plans are totally solid"

"Can't you adjust your priorities? After all, I *am* Jack's mother."

"Nope. Hope you get it worked out. Gotta go. Talk to you tomorrow." This was *her* night. No one had the power to spoil the second Friday of the month.

Elizabeth drew in a long breath and smiled. She'd thought of nothing else for the last thirty days. Cinderella never had it this good. Her heart raced as she glided into the master bedroom and settled onto the king-sized bed.

Her red cocktail dress hung in the back of her closet. Her overnight bag, packed with a black-silk nightgown, lace teddy, and bubble bath, was carefully hidden under the bed. Tonight she'd devour *him.*

By seven P.M., the red satin dress draped her shoulders. Glossy dark brown hair touched the middle of her bare back. A diamond pendent rested against the curves of her breasts. She allowed herself one final glance in the mirror and beamed. Time to go.

Elizabeth sauntered into the bar of the Carlton Ritz. She gazed around the room. Impressive. She recognized him immediately. He'd actually emailed a current photo. His muscles fought the restrictions of his black blazer. His blond hair and blue eyes— perfect against his golden tan. His long legs, bent at the knees, swung from the barstool. She preferred tall men. He met all of her criteria. He sipped from one of the two glasses of white wine, his eyes focused on the doorway. She drank in his anticipation.

He dropped off the stool and waved her over. "You must be Candy. You're more beautiful than your online photo. Love that dress. Red's my favorite color." She warmed, as he slipped a forceful arm around her waist, and brushed his lips against her cheek.

Elizabeth leaned in, cupped his ear, and whispered, "Nice to finally meet you." His cheeks turned crimson. "I found your profile page intriguing. Wow," she purred.

He drew her even closer and closed his eyes. Taking a deep breath, he inhaled her essence. "Your scent— fresh, clean, and floral. You belong in a butterfly patch, surrounded by beautiful flowers swaying in the breeze."

Elizabeth clasped his right-hand, pulled his fingers to her lips and gently kissed each one. "I'm looking forward to this evening."

"Candy. Let's toast to our evening. Champagne, right?"

"Yes. Perfect."

He raised his fluted glass of bubbling Tattinger. "To the most amazing woman I've ever met."

She leaned against his long, buff torso and placed her arm into his. "Let's settle at our table and get to know each other before…Well, you know."

He bent down, and placed his thumb against her face. He traced her cheekbone with his touch. "I hope to know you *well*. But first, dinner. The chef here is famous for his culinary art. You must be famished."

"I am. The anticipation of our date filled my hunger all day—now I'm starved. I do want to know all about you, too. Do you go by Robert?"

"My close friends call me Robbie. And you will certainly be one of my best friends after tonight."

Gazing downward, she fluttered her eyelids. "Then Robbie, it is."

Once seated, the waiter handed each of them a leather menu, offered hot rolls, and disappeared like a Vegas magician.

"Candy, tell me what brought you to the Every Second Friday website?"

Elizabeth raised her gaze to his and beamed. "I've been restless all my life. Lots of boyfriends, but no one who could hold my interest. Even as a small child, I raced my bike, jumped the curbs, and loved the taste of fear. I'm an adrenalin-junky. When I met my husband, he actually *got me.* He provides me the freedom to be myself. I love him deeply for that."

"Does he require the same *freedoms*?"

"Not really. But he gets reward points for allowing me to be myself. It actually works out well." She cleared her throat. "What about your home life? Does your wife know you are here with me tonight?"

"Yes, of course. We have no secrets. She understands me, too."

Elizabeth beamed. "This will be a lovely evening."

Robbie lifted his drink and replied, "A toast to wonderful spouses."

The following morning Robbie awoke early. He tiptoed into the shower and returned twenty minutes later, bathed, shaved, and hair perfect. Humming, he picked up the phone and ordered breakfast for two. Stepping closer to the king-sized bed, he bent over and kissed her closed eyelids.

"Candy, my sweet, we must soon end our date. Breakfast is on its way."

Nestled in the feather pillows, Elizabeth mumbled, "It can't be morning already."

"Afraid so. I have to get to work by ten."

"Okay. I'll shower and be ready to eat in thirty minutes. Wish we had all day to spend together."

"Yep. Me too. But you know the club rules." He gave her a gentle tap on her backside and kissed her behind the ear." Next month, same place, same time? You can call me *Bryan.* What will I call you?"

"Look for *Sandy.*"

"Will you wear black for me?"

"Black, it is."

Saturday evening, Jack flew into the house, grabbed Elisabeth, and kissed her hungrily. "I sure missed you, Babe."

Elizabeth playfully pushed him away, and smiled. "Slow down, Mister. Do I know you?"

He scooped her into his arms and marched to their bedroom. "Yep. You know me very well. Jack is my name. Robbie's my other, and Robbie is still hungry for Candy."

She chuckled.

"Good, because Candy really wanted a second evening with Robbie."

Jack grinned. "Sure do love this new club you found for us. Is there one for every Friday?"

"That's my tiger. I'll check into it later. Shall we skip dinner?"

A Lesson Learned

by

Joyce M. Ross

The little angel sat atop the bureau, staring down at the sleeping infant. Legs akimbo, elbows on knees, she glanced at her mentor, who dozed in the hardback rocker. Head back, mouth open, a slight snore escaped his lips.

"I don't get it," she said aloud, although only the dozing angel could hear her. As he opened his eyes, she continued. "This is so boring. All he does is sleep. How am I supposed to learn my duties when he doesn't do anything?"

Her elder looked at her and winked. "Well," he said, "God knows what he's doing. I think you'll find this is a good assignment for you." He glanced at an imaginary watch. "Oh, look how late it is! I'll be going now. I'll catch up with you in a few years."

"What? Wait! No, don't leave…" But the elder was gone, and the angel looked in panic at the baby, quietly sleeping in his crib. "Well," she said, "Maybe I can handle it." She settled down and relaxed.

Years sped by. The young angel became quite fond of her charge, and found as he grew older, he was harder to keep out of trouble. She had to let the occasional trial and tribulation enter his life, or he would not learn any lessons—or so she had been taught in angel school.

When her charge reached puberty, he was a very attractive young man, tall and broad shouldered, with curly black hair and a smile that warmed the hearts of teenage girls. Unfortunately, he seemed determined to break many of those hearts.

The angel didn't like where her charge was headed. He was not as callous as he appeared, yet he seemed to delight in tormenting the female sex. When she heard him bragging about being a 'player', she knew it was time she stepped up and did her angelic duty. Unfortunately, she didn't know what she could do.

She beseeched her elder, whom she had not seen in years. She wasn't surprised when she received no answer.

"I'll take care of this, and if I do wrong, well, I'm sure they'll let me know."

She altered her appearance and inspected herself in a mirror. A tall, willowy blonde, with a slight upturned nose and dimple in one cheek stared back at her. She practiced a flirty smile and a quirk of an eyebrow. Yes, she would do. Just the type her young man seemed to favor.

Checking the time, she figured her charge would be leaving football practice and headed to the mall. Her intention was to interfere with his plans for the evening after he arrived there, and looking for his next conquest.

She waited inside a teen fashion store, her arms laden with shopping bags, purse over her shoulder, cell phone in hand, ready to put to her ear. Wearing a tight pink sweater and short skirt, she didn't intend to take any chances he could miss her. She shook her head, her long blonde hair flowing in heady curls down her back. One man glanced toward her and walked into a nearby mannequin.

Her charge strolled through the mall entrance, his buddy Joel at his side. They were laughing.

She bustled out of the store, bags fluttering on her arm, cell phone to her ear, a distressed look on her face as she flung herself in the path of the two teenagers. She collided directly into her charge, knocking him down and herself as well, her purchases and cell phone flying across the floor.

"Oh! I am so sorry!" She cried. As they picked up her items, she blushed and words flooded from her mouth. "I was in a hurry. That man, I think he's following me." She glanced over her shoulder toward the center of the mall, where an elderly man sat patiently.

"Well, there was a man. I know there was. And he scared me." She stuffed her purchases back into their sacks, and with the help of the young men, got to her feet.

Joel picked up her cell phone and handed it to her. "I think I'll go on," he said, looking at his companion. "I'll catch up with you later."

As his friend walked away, her charge turned toward her, and offered his hand. "My name's Jared. What's your name?"

Nervous, still looking around for the scary man, she replied, "Angela. I'm sorry I knocked you down."

"Oh, that's all right." He looked approvingly at her face, her hair, and down her figure. "Actually, you can knock me down anytime." As she smiled, he continued, "If you're finished shopping, can I walk you to your car?"

"That would be nice."

The next two weeks passed quickly. Jared became more enamored of Angela and she continued to use her feminine wiles to reel him in. When Jared pressured Angela for sex, she decided it was time to finish the lesson she had started.

They were parked in a dark, cozy spot, when Angela pushed Jared back, telling him they needed to talk.

"Talk?" Jared pulled back. "About what?"

"About us," Angela answered.

"What about us? You know I adore you, sweetie. And I think you're pretty crazy over me, too." He smiled and moved in for another kiss.

"Do you love me?" Angela asked.

"What?"

"You want to have sex with me. Do you love me?"

Jared looked away. "Yeah, of course I love you. How could you think otherwise?"

"Well, I don't love you. And I can't lie. So I think you better take me home now."

Stunned, Jared stared at Angela, then turned and started the engine. As they drove homeward, he said, "I thought you liked me."

"I do like you. Love you, no. Besides, I've heard about how you're a player. And I can't believe what you say, knowing that." She looked out the window as he pulled up in front of the house she claimed was her home. "Besides, there's someone else."

"Someone else?" He stopped the car at the curb and looked at her in shock. "How could there be someone else? We've only been going out a couple of weeks!"

"It hurts, doesn't it?" She looked at him with wise, knowing eyes. "Maybe next time, when you break a heart, you'll think about how much it hurts that girl. And maybe you won't string her along." She reached for the door handle.

"Wait." His quiet tone made her look at him. "So that was your plan. To hurt Jared as he had hurt so many others, so he would learn his lesson, and grow into a responsible adult."

Angela got out of the car. Jared got out also, and walked around to stand in front of her.

"What do you mean, to hurt Jared? You are Jared. What kind of stupid joke is this?"

"I'm right, aren't I?" He looked solemnly at her. "You were trying to teach him a lesson."

"So what if I was?"

He leaned against the car, crossed his arms, watching her. "A new angel has to have a lot of basic training. You have just passed one of your first tests - to see how far you would let your charge go, before you led him back to where he belonged."

Angela stared at him, jaw slack. Reasoning began to dawn. "Who are you?"

He smiled and moved away from the car. Large silvery wings slowly fanned out behind him. "I am one of your teachers."

She leaned against the car for support. "I didn't know. They didn't say anything about this in class."

"Yeah, there are some things they don't tell you."

Angela was thoughtful. "So, if you are Jared, now, does Jared even exist? Has this whole lesson, been just that, a lesson?"

"Oh no, Jared does exist, and you will continue to watch over him. For the duration of this lesson, though, I have periodically used him to test you."

He leaned toward her and kissed her on the cheek. "But cheer up, kiddo. You did very well. Maybe I'll see you another time."

He winked and disappeared, leaving her standing alone in the street.

Beach Dogs
by
Mary Coley

"Hey, mon. Welcome to Jamaica."

Fred and Basil, two of the many beach dogs I've come to know on Treasure Beach, speak with a rhythm like all Jamaicans. Behind the words, the music of the island pulses and the sea rolls.

I watch Basil and Fred from the porch of my vacation beach house as they chase each other in and out of the bubbling surf of the Caribbean ocean, tumbling and leaping in a happy dog dance. This life is so different from the way I lived before. Here, I feel no urge to get involved or take a stand on anything. I'm free to come and go as I please. The most intense I ever get is when I'm watching these dogs.

Fred is larger than Basil and has long legs. His curly fur is brown, white, cream, and tan. It curls over his body and his long tail wags so that the fringe of swinging hair strews water droplets all around. His jaw is open in a smile most of the time.

Basil, whose short coat is white, doesn't jump as high as Fred over the waves. Quick and well-toned with a black face, Basil looks like a dog from the Terrier Group of the Westminster Dog Show. He prances around the houses lining Treasure Beach as if he is in the show ring.

Basil believes the beach and all of the people on it belong to him. Give him a kind word, a scratch behind the ears, and Basil will think he 'owns' you. He'll snap at Fred if his friend's tail wags too much or if he pushes too close to someone Basil 'owns.' Basil especially dislikes it when Fred's coat is wet and clotted with sand. Basil is very careful about his appearance.

I've been in Jamaica for several months now, watching these dogs. Some island visitors seem to think there are too many dogs running around. Some of them belong to the vacation families; others are unwanted. Personally, I think they're all good dogs. The pack outcasts the bad ones; they slink away to the interior of the island.

At night, when the beach bonfires have died down and the people have gone inside, heads ringing with Caribbean rum and songs, the dogs gather around the glowing coals and tell stories.

Off in the distance, one last band with a steel drum plays a final tribute to Bob Marley. "Let's get together and feel all right . . ." the crowd sings.

Learning the stories of these dogs has taken time. They've come to me piecemeal, gathered from conversations overheard at the women's art cooperative where they sell their crafts, jewelry and clothing, or at the corner market. One part of Basil's story was told to me by the cook at Hebare's Rum Shack, where I went one hot August afternoon to escape the sun and dream about the slightly cooler days to come.

I would imagine that Fred loves the story Basil tells about how he came to live on Jamaica's Treasure Beach, especially since Fred plays a major part. Basil probably tells the story to every new dog that races onto the beach after a Frisbee or trudges onto the wet, packed sand, dirty and hungry.

"I came to Treasure Beach years ago, after escaping from my shipping crate at the Montego Bay airport," Basil begins. "My handler was taking me out of my crate for a walk on the grass when I made a break for it. He wasn't the smartest handler I'd ever had. He should have grabbed my collar before he opened the crate's gate."

At this point, I see Basil lifting his left hind foot and scratching his ear before settling onto his haunches. "I was boiling mad. My ride in the luggage compartment of the plane had been horrible. Two airsick cats in the crates across from me puked and yowled the entire trip.

"Riding in planes was a large part of my life until then," he continues. "I'd be flying from one dog show to another. Shampoos, haircuts and nail trims. Tiresome. I'd had enough." Basil yawns and stands up, performing 'downward facing dog' (the yoga move) with precision before sitting again.

"So, I hightailed it out of Montego Bay, or MoBay as we say here in Jamaica. I headed cross-country at a steady trot."

At this point in Basil's story, Fred's ears perk up.

"About two hours out of Mo Bay, I saw a furry, brown dog in the roadway, his hind legs stretched behind him. This stranger was ready to start a new life. His name was Fred."

Fred grins and drops his head onto his outstretched front paws.

The next part of Basil's story I learned from Etienne, the boy on the bicycle. He rides around this part of the island picking up bits of metal and cardboard for his mother to use in her 'junk yard art' business. Etienne speaks in Basil's voice with an English accent.

"My new friend, Fred, took one last look at the tin-roofed shack of the chicken farmer he'd been living with for the past year, rolled over and wriggled, scratching his back in the gritty gravel. Then, we trotted together down the road. In another hour or so we were at Treasure Beach."

The bicyclist expands the story. Still in Basil's accent he says, "This beach is a great place to live. People are plentiful and so are scraps – and compost piles. We stay because of those compost piles. Except for an occasional bone Suzette slips us from the kitchen of Calabash House Bed and Breakfast, we have both become vegetarians."

I laugh and scratch Basil's smooth head. Etienne laughs too, revealing strong white teeth, nourished by the abundant papaya, coconut, mango and bananas of Treasure Beach, Jamaica.

If I were on the beach with the dogs by the dying bonfire, I could imagine dog questions and Basil's responses.

"Don't you miss your other life?" One of the audience dogs yips.

Basil gazes at the blue Caribbean Sea and shakes his head. "I miss watching TV sometimes, especially the British dramas on the public channel. A good hunting scene pricks my interest and stirs my blood."

"You don't miss the dog shows?" Another dog whines.

Basil snorts. "No. What dog would ever miss being picked up by his tail and lifted to the judging stand? Not me for sure."

A little black dog yips. "Fred, don't you miss the farm?"

Fred lifts his head. "Nothin' to miss." His head drops back down onto his paws.

"Anyone up for a good run?" Basil asks. They race away, running fast so the foaming wave fingers can't grab their toes.

Basil is a good friend; he knows Fred doesn't want to talk about his former lives, and especially not the years with the chicken farmer. Kind of like me, and my former lives.

I've heard about that farmer. Fred probably shared the tale with Basil one night, very late, while a sliver of silver moon crept across the sky.

"I still be missin' the family," he moans to Basil. "Them I lived with as a pup. The boy loved me. He did. Yah. He did and I give him me youth–me first year."

A little whine escapes from Fred. According to the story I'd heard, he'd hung around the empty house for a while, waiting for his family to come back, but hours turned into days and he got hungry. The chicken farmer lived only a few miles from the family's vacation home. Truth was, the farmer didn't give Fred enough to eat. Fred lost his puppy fat and learned not to eat chicken bones.

Fred closes his eyes, and lets the *shhh-shhhh-shhhhh* of the surf and the warm sand lull him to sleep.

I lie on my beach towel nearby; the warm breeze and the compliant sand pull the last bit of residual tension from my body. It occurs to me that Basil, and Fred, and the island have all begun to own me.

Some hours later, the sky brightens, turning shades of grayish pink as the morning sun peeps above the horizon.

Basil yawns. Fred lifts his head, rolls over and stretches, extending all four legs into the air. I prop my head up on one arm and watch, imagining their conversation.

"Yo, Basil. Hey, mon? Wanna run down to the wat'r, see who's about?"

"In a bit, Fred."

"How about the compost pile? Think there'll be anything new today?"

"Probably."

"Mmmm. Yah. Mango and papaya rind, and browned cabbage." Fred gets up, walks a few steps to the nearest yard and throws himself down, twisting his body to give his back a good scratch. "Say, heard there'll be soccer again on Sunday. I be goin' there fo' sure, yah."

"That'll be good." Basil's mouth stretches wide open in a yawn.

"I feelin' the need to jump the waves, mon. Maybe Doobie, Ralph or Nappie be there a'ready."

"Cheerio, then." Basil stretches out on a narrow strip of lush grass in the yard.

"I goin,' mon." Fred trots away.

Basil drops his head and rests it on his front paws, watching me.

I sit up and stretch, peer up at the clear blue sky. Just another day in paradise.

Basil and I walk down the dirt and gravel road next to the grassy fields. I hear voices twittering, coming toward us.

Three ladies appear. Their laughter tickles the air. People wags his short tail. People. More people for him to own.

He dashes to them, dancing in a circle as they laugh and reach to pet him. He doesn't let them, yet.

"Is this your dog? He's so cute. Does he do tricks?" One of them asks me.

Basil prances and dances some more, rising up on his hind legs to show them he has wonderful balance and strength. He rolls on the soft grass beside the road. They are all smiling, mouths open, calling him.

Finally, he lets them touch him. Their scents swirl in the hot dry air–lavender soap, lilac and a fruity mix of mango and papaya with pineapple undertones. The fourth one simply smells like a human.

One of them touches Basil's neck, expecting to find a collar, and she does. The collar is blue leather faded to white with the passage of years. "He's so cute. You've trained him well."

I smile. "Someone did. He lives on the beach," I say.

They mutter and look around. "Poor dog. He's lost," one says.

Basil barks and backs away from her. I go around them in the road and continue toward the center of the village. Basil scampers after me.

Back on the beach, Basil and I sit on the wet sand. He scratches at the underneath part of his neck, where his faded collar rubs. Behind us, in one of the pink, green and blue beach houses where the back door has been left open, the radio blares another Marley chorus, "Every little thing is gonna be all right."

So why do I have a bad feeling in the center of my chest, a feeling like I used to have before a board meeting when the CEO was about to make a decision that directly affected me?

Basil stretches his back into the up-dog yoga position. Fifty yards away, Fred stands at a rocky section of beach, nose in a rock pool, tail wagging. Fred snorts and jumps back barking.

"Found a blenny, no doubt," I think.

Blenny. I love the word for the rock pool fish just as much as Fred loves to search for them. The contest is whether the fish or Fred can remain still the longest, each waiting for the other to move. Fred usually wins.

Basil yawns and stretches out on the sand, pushing his belly down into the grainy warmth. Seconds later, he jumps up and peers down at the sand, lifting first one foot and then the other. Basil backs away and then dashes down the beach where Fred is still snorting and jumping by the rock pool.

Basil barks. I can translate. He's saying, "Hey, Fred. Come see this!"

Fred leaps into the air and twists, then lands on all four feet. "Yo, mon. Me be busy. See that blenny move, yah, sure did."

Basil takes off, runs back down the beach toward me. "Now, Fred. Come on!"

Fred looks from the rock pool to his friend, and then races after him.

Basil points with his nose at the indentation in the sand where he had been lying moments before. "It was right here. The sand moved!"

Fred sniffs the spot, his nose working as his tail wags back and forth. "Not seein' nothin,' bro," he snorts. Fred snuffles some more, examining the sand. "Yo," he finally growls. "Somethin' there. Way down."

Basil blinks and backs away, his short, little tail drooping.

Fred barks. "Let's dig!"

"Not me," Basil yips as he dashes away.

Fred stares at the sand a few minutes longer. The sand remains still. "Ol' Basil be losin' it. Nothin' happenin' here." He races away after Basil. You could always count on Fred to join a game of chase.

I wander into town for dinner at Hebare's Rum Shack. Word has made it around town that Hebare himself had caught a slew of fish on the Black River early this morning and is frying them up. I join my friends at a community table and sip at a bottle of Red Stripe.

The ladies Basil and I had encountered that afternoon bustled in soon after. By then, the single tables are filled, so they join us at the community table.

"Say," one of them says, not looking at anyone in particular. "I've seen lots of dogs on the beaches. To whom do they belong? Aren't they a problem?"

Jake, a British ex-pat, snorts. "No problem to me. Botherin' you?"

"I think that little white one is a missing show dog. His picture is on the internet. Lost in Jamaica, four years ago. There's a reward."

Several heads at the table turn. I keep my head down, finish my beer and take my fish dinner to go.

Basil, Fred and I walk along the beach as the orange sun drops into the sea.

Fred pushes his nose along the ground and although Basil walks more or less in a straight line, Fred zigzags, following the smells and the little sand crab tracks.

We pass the very spot where earlier today Basil had felt movement beneath him as he lay next to me on the sand.

"Yo!" Fred yaps.

"What is it?" Basil yips.

"The sand! It's a-movin,' like ya said!" Fred howls.

The sand ripples, small sections pushing up then dropping. A bit of beach the size of a rock pool is moving.

Basil freezes, legs stiff.

Fred leans over the swirling sand, sniffing.

The sand churns open beneath him. He leaps into the air and away.

The sandy beach comes alive with baby turtles. Basil hops about as little creatures scurry toward the foamy edge of the retreating sea.

The sky fills with birds; gulls, terns and petrels dive bomb the seething sand, snatch up the little turtles and flap away. Dozens and dozens more birds arrive every second.

"Sea turtles!" Fred yips. "And there be more!"

Basil and I glance down the beach. Tiny creatures scamper everywhere, but the birds are picking them off.

"They're outnumbered!" Basil barks. "Help them!"

He and Fred race along the beach, barking and jumping at the birds so the little turtles can scramble toward the foamy surf.

I race toward the sea, too, waving my arms and screaming as tiny sea turtles scuttle past. "Run for it, sea babies!"

The next morning, the sky rumbles.

Basil opens one eye and looks up. What has happened to the sun? Gray and black clouds tumble and roll from one side of the sky to the other.

I maneuver myself into the hammock on the beach cabin's porch.

"Fred!" Basil yips.

"Yah. I'm right here." Fred is snuffling through a pile of dirt and compost next door. He snorts and jumps, then rubs his nose with one paw. "Nasty crab that was." He trots over to Basil. "Gonna come a blow."

The two dogs leap onto the porch. Sheets of rain slice through the heavens and down through the mango trees. The drops beat on the tin roof of the cabin, flung by a relentless wind. The roof vibrates. More heavy drops crash down.

The dogs rest their heads on their paws. If living at the beach has taught us anything, it is that storms come and storms go. Certain months the storms rage more often, or last for hours. But the storms always end and the sun blazes. We are willing to wait.

A wonderful smell flows from the ocean after a storm. The air, fresh and heaven-scented, caresses the beach neighborhood. All kinds of things show up on the beach after a storm. Creatures from the deep, floats from fishing nets, and even odd things from far away which had been bobbing around in the ocean forever.

Today, the ocean has tossed the frame of an old car onto the beach, its painted skin rubbed whale-gray by sand. The men of the town gather around it, but the other dogs and their barking draw me, Basil and Fred down the beach.

Every dog in town has gathered, including Doobie, Ralph and Nappie. They bark and dance around a large pool at the old reef rocks.

"What is it?" Basil yips.

"Never seen nothin' like it," Doobie yaps.

"It's a . . . it's a SEA MONSTER," Ralph howls.

Pink and purple-gray and big and blubbery and stretched out in all directions, the creature fills the bottom of the biggest pool and overflows onto the rocky edge. A giant eye stares up at us. The eye rolls, looking from Doobie to Basil, Fred and me.

A tentacle lifts from the water.

"Run!" Doobie yelps.

Even Basil, who usually isn't frightened of anything, takes off, leaving me alone at the rocky pool with the octopus.

It takes a while for me to get the creature out of the pool, over the rocks and back to the sea, but eventually it disappears into the waves. The shore birds circle over my head, dropping to the sand for an occasional crab and calling into the wind.

I walk back up the beach. Where are the dogs? The uncomfortable feeling in my chest grows into a throbbing pain.

I step through the beach access cut between two of the houses and onto the road. The hot air caresses my head and a fly lands on my hand. I flick it away and start for town.

The white van is parked across the street from the arts cooperative. Two men in white uniforms laugh, slapping one another on the arm as they peer inside the back of the van. Although I'm still two blocks away, I hear the muffled yelps and cries of the beach dogs.

The English ladies peer into the van and point.

"That one there," the tall lady with the straw hat says.

I close my eyes as I come nearer and let the cries lead me. There's Basil, and Fred, Doobie and Nappie, and others I don't know by voice. I stumble in a rut and lose one worn flip-flop.

"I lured them all here, you owe me. Give me that white one," the tall woman instructed one of the fat workers.

I circle the truck, blending in as I always do, with my tanned skin, graying ponytail, faded cropped top and shorts. The ladies are watching the dogs; no one is watching me.

I slip into the cab of the van. The key is in the ignition; the engine is running. I ease off the parking brake and push down clutch and accelerator as I shove the gear shift into first.

[187]

The van moves; the ladies and the workers shout. I zoom down the street, leaving a cloud of dust behind me.

At the road to the soccer field, I hang a right. A block farther, under the shade of the largest tree, I stop the van and get out.

The dogs are barking. They quiet when I begin to open the individual cages. One by one, they leap from the van and run in every direction.

Basil and Fred wait for me on the far side of the field. Their tails wag as we cut through the goat field and head toward my beach house.

Somewhere in the distance, a local band practices another Bob Marley song, this one is something about a sheriff. It ends with ". . . freedom come my way."

I think about freedom, my life on this island, and my dogs.

Come Die With Me
by
Donna Welch Jones

Clouds below me puffed their softness into multiple shapes. Rays of sun perforated the spaces between them sending spikes of light into Heaven. I waited—apprehensive—unsure that I deserved this celestial place. Reaching out my hand I grasped love, and air swirled joy around me.

I felt wrapped in calmness, except for a fear remnant lodged in my brain. The fragment didn't disappear, with other earthly worries, when my heart stopped beating.

Saint Peter let me in, but kept his distance as he warned me not to wander from the gate's shadow. The structure is a mile high. Rubies, emeralds, and diamonds are engrained in the gold posts.

As I waited, the gate opened. A woman in a nun's habit appeared. As soon as her foot touched the silver stones of Heaven her black garment transformed to pure white, and her back sprouted pearl-embedded wings. She flowed into a light far beyond me. The calmness that swaddled me loosened. My

[189]

instinctual fear expanded. An explanation rose from my heart—God was undecided.

Peter tossed a gray cloak toward me. After I put it on he motioned to pull up the hood. A breeze pushed me forward. The swift air stopped, and my body anchored in one spot. The light forced my head down and eyes shut.

"Susan, you stand before God because your earthly life was moral, but your service to God inadequate. In order to receive elevation to Angel status you must choose two others from humanity to enter heaven with you. Your three souls must merge to form an Angel worthy of God's home."

"Follow Peter to the transition room. You will determine who among your friends and family will die on earth so you can enter Heaven."

The hexagonal room allowed only enough space to stand upright. Glass walls surrounded me. At my left was a giant magnifier. I manipulated the lever to focus on earth. I reached into the abyss certain I could touch the treetops, but my hand floated above them.

Peter extended one arm in the door, and turned the gage to pull a location in front of my eyes.

I reached out again—trying to pick a daffodil from the church garden. My hand boomeranged, and smacked my face.

My daughters and grandchildren exited a long black limousine. Now I understood. God sent me to my own funeral to choose who will die.

I recalled Grandmother saying that people died in threes. If one friend or relative expired then two others soon followed. I thought it a coincidence, but now I knew the truth. Like me, if the first dead wasn't a totally righteous person he couldn't enter heaven without the combined goodness of two others.

I diminished the intensity of the magnifier, and viewed rows of heads from the back of the church. Most straight, some bowing, a couple turned with lips whispering in the next ear. A granddaughter bent with head in her hands. My daughters held hands. Siblings scrunched together with nieces and nephews. My lady friends congregated at the back. Uncles, aunts, cousins, and acquaintances all came to say farewell.

My instructions were to choose the two people whose souls will merge with mine for eternity. Within days after my funeral the chosen two will die, and be lifted to heaven. I choose who dies.

I recalibrated the magnifier, and honed in on each mourner's face.

If I chose my daughters, who gave me joy in life, my grandchildren would be motherless.

If my nieces and nephews were dead, my brother and sister would be left with broken hearts.

Peter opened the door, "Your decision?"

"Hell."

He nodded. I followed him to the gate. Strikes of light reflected from the sun below to the golden bars. As I stepped out, the silver stones of Heaven ended. My body swirled downward through a storm of rocks and ten-inch varmints. Their pointed tongues brought blood oozing from my pores as they licked my body on the downward spiral.

Rock tremored as my body hit a smoky pit. Black puffs of ash surrounded me. Smoke invaded my insides then escaped through eyes, ears, and nose. Sharp teeth clamped the back of my neck, and carried me toward a fiery throne.

Creature's teeth pulled from my neck. I felt highlights of blood seeping into my hair. His paw pushed into my side. I rolled toward the Devil.

"Creature, what have you brought? The spit that erupted with the Devil's words scalded my chest."

"A soul for his highness."

The tightening of the Devil's face sent blood clots dripping from his nose. "She doesn't smell right."

Creature bowed his furry snout to the ground, and looked at the Devil through hairy eyes. "She was thrown out of Heaven."

"There's a disgusting stench about her. Prepare her properly or I shall sever your ugly head."

Creature inserted his teeth into my bloody neck holes. Four-inch splinters punctured my body as he drug me across wood planks to a small room.

"The Devil will curse your family on earth if you don't bring two humans to Hell to absorb your smell of righteousness. Your soul will intertwine with theirs forever. If you're a fool, and bring in two murderers, you'll reside in the hottest level of Hell. If your choices are less evil, your pain will be commensurate."

He handed me a laser, and shut the door. The small hexagon room, with a huge earth magnifier, was like the one in Heaven. I started my search.

First, I saw a teenager stealing an old man's money. One zap of my magic laser, and he'd burn in Hell.

Next, I zeroed in on a movie theater. A mean girl cornered a frail peer in the restroom. Her words screeched into my head. "You're so ugly I should throw up on your face."

My attention strayed to a glimmer of light from a second story window. A child's whisper "please don't" magnified to a scream as it reached my ears. I focused the machine, and looked in the window.

He stood above the naked child. His hands grasped her ankles, and pulled her legs apart. I aimed the laser toward his head, and pushed the button. His grip released. The child ran toward her neighbor's house. Blood and particles of brain burst from the abuser's ears.

I moved the magnifier. A woman ran softly, her feet barely touched the ground. A box padded in bubble wrap held firmly in both hands. Her eyes darted from side-to-side. She paused in the alley behind the Federal Building. She jimmied the lock. I zeroed in on her activity through the window. A bomb came into view as she uncurled the wrap. I aimed my weapon at the package. The bomber and the empty building burst violently into the air.

"You have finished," Creature stated. "Since you chose the worst of the worst you're damned to burn in the lowest level of Hell. Follow me."

The steps went ever downward as flames shot toward me, then swerved as they reached my face. The lower I went the higher the screeching—the louder the moans. Smoke lodged in my throat, and soot coughed out.

My victims, now my partners, the child abuser and the bomber stood in a pit of red and yellow flames. Their eyebrows and hair already burned to a black crispy crud. Their hoarse yells for help echoed from the walls, and back into the holes where their ears once were.

"They never burn up, but stay on fire forever, as is your fate," Creature assured me.

"Join your soul mates." Creature yelled, then bit into my neck, and flung me toward the pit.

Smoke held me above the flames for a second, then I felt gravity pulling downward. A clawed hand grabbed, then dropped me. When I looked up I saw the Devil sitting on his fiery throne.

"I'm quite pleased," he said. "The two earthly specimens you found have the most marvelous fragrance of evil. You're my huntress. Each day you must go into the small room, and search for sinners."

"I will bring you the worst evil in humanity," I promised.

The Devil's mushy blood-face looked elated, "Go now and search. An abundance of hate, prejudice, and cruelty unified in Hell—my perfect world."

Creature followed me in the hexagon room. "My sense of smell is better than the Devil's. Too much smoke has accumulated in his head."

I smoothed his furry back. "What are you implying my pet?"

"Just thought I caught a whiff of kindness when I passed you, but must be mistaken." Creature curled at my feet.

I focused the magnifier on earth, and pulled images closer. Peace surrounded me as I zapped twenty child abusers, five murderers and six wife beaters—a good day in Hell.

Going Home
by
J. A. Kimmel

Only a few more steps, thought Carl. Once I make it to the door, everything will be all right. I'll be home, and Helen will take care of me. Fifty-six years of waking beside her. Though his whole body ached, he willed himself to keep pressing forward until he finally grasped the knob.

As he entered the house, he heard the sounds of running water and rattling pans.

Is that goulash I smell?

"Carl?" Helen called.

Trying to remove his jacket further sapped his strength.

"Let me help you," she offered, walking toward him. "How are you this evening?"

"I feel like I just ploughed the west forty with a pocket comb on my hands and knees," he answered, attempting to smile. The effort was too much.

She took his hand, and her lips brushed against his stubbly cheek.

"I hope you at least feel up to a shave, Mr. Bauer," she teased, her blue eyes sparkling, reminding him of a summer sky.

In her eyes, he saw the church where they met as children, and, later, married. He saw their daughter, Elizabeth, and their nieces and nephews, being baptized, confirmed, and married there. He saw their grandchildren playing in the grassy church cemetery, where tall trees, planted after the first burials, provided shade. Adults were wandering from marker to marker, placing flowers on family graves.

He caught sight of Helen bending low in the shade of a decades-old cedar. A breeze ruffled the hemline of her skirt and played upon the curls framing her face. She was tucking a bunch of garden flowers into an urn beside one of the oldest headstones. Weathered and leaning, it bore German inscriptions engraved into granite.

There rested his father, who claimed his parcel of Oklahoma in the Land Rush of 1889. A stout, God-fearing man, he built the church, board by board, with other settlers of European origin. An immigrant, too, his wife rested beside him, along with their twin infant sons, victims of Scarlet Fever. When his five surviving children were old enough to take up the plough or to marry, he divided his land among them. In keeping with the new homeland, their markers displayed English text. Four double headstones commemorated Carl's brothers and sisters and their spouses. A fifth, also double, displayed two hearts linked together, but the stone carver had left space for one final inscription.

"Mr. Bauer? Mr. Bauer, time for your medicine," insisted an unfamiliar voice, disrupting the images.

Don't go, Helen.

A hand cradled, then lifted his head, pressing a cup against his dry lips. He sipped, swallowing the cool wetness that, somehow, didn't soothe. As his head sank back into the pillow, he became aware of the catheter and the antiseptic odor threatening to smother him. Retreating footsteps heralded the click of the door.

Gradually, he realized that someone was holding his hand.

His eyes flickered open. In the dim glow of the monitor's lights, he made out several flower bouquets and a middle-aged woman sitting beside his bed with her head bowed.

"You still here, Lizzie?" he rasped, his voice a whisper.

"Yes, Daddy."

So am I. Goin' on four years.

"Sure you don't want a shave?" she asked hopefully.

"Maybe tomorrow."

He studied her brown hair falling in waves, her square jaw mirroring his. "You've got your mama's eyes."

She sniffled. "I miss her."

"Me, too."

For a while, he fought the weariness. Tried to stay with her. *Bunkin' 130-pound bales of hay in the barn would be easier.* At last, his eyes fell closed.

"Daddy," Lizzie's voice quavered, "I love you. When you see Mama . . . tell her I love her."

He could only nod.

Lizzie's small hand trembled in his palm, and, so, he did what he had done many times during her childhood to calm her fear of the dark. He wrapped his fingers around hers and squeezed.

As she squeezed back, he heard her ragged intake of breath.

Then once again, the door—now, fully open—beckoned.

A brilliant light surrounded and filled him, drawing him toward something that was infinitely larger than himself, yet part of himself—something that was pure love.

Home.

He was going home. Helen was waiting for him.

Cyberstalk

by

Gloria Teague

The letters glowing on the computer monitor cast a reflection in the obsidian pupils of his eyes.

For him, for this moment in time, nothing else existed. He didn't hear the television droning on in the living room, the hum of the refrigerator, or the hiss of the fan on the computer terminal.

Mac: *Hello darling*

CelticRose: *Mac!*

Mac: *Yes Rose, it's me, the one that misses you so.*

CelticRose: *Oh, I love the way you speak! It's so romantic!*

Mac: *I'm happy I made you smile.*

CelticRose: *Sweetheart, you just don't know what you do to me! <blushing>*

Mac: *Rose, your soft beauty takes my breath away. I lie awake at night, wanting you, longing for you.*

CelticRose: *---→ CelticRose blushes.*

Mac: *Don't blush, for it is the truth. Surely a desire for your love shouldn't cause embarrassment? It's really not my intention to make you uncomfortable. I just want to share my feelings with you.*

CelticRose: *Oh Mac, you're getting me hot!*

His grimace turned into a sneer. It was working, just as it always did. The stupid cow was buying this and he didn't even have to try.

Mac: *Beautiful, sexy, desirable CelticRose! I want you so badly. I can't sleep at night for imagining you lying beside me, or shall I dare say it, beneath me?*

CelticRose: *Mac! Lol*

Mac: *What my love? Am I going too fast? Am I scaring you? If I am, just say the word and I'll stop this second.*

CelticRose: *No, you're not scaring me, honey, just making me feel things my own husband never could.*

Mac: *Oh Rose, a woman as lovely as you should be loved every minute of every day. If you were mine, I'd show you how much I wanted you.*

CelticRose: *Oh Mac, you really know how to get a girl excited!*

Mac: *I'm so happy I can please you, even if only in this small way.*

CelticRose: *No, in a BIG way, sweet, sexy Mac!*

Mac: **Rose,** *I want you. NOW. I want to visualize making love to you. Can we do that, my beautiful Rose? May I love you tonight?*

CelticRose: Y*esssss. Oh please love me, Mac!*

Mac: *Is **Hubby** asleep?*

CelticRose: *Yes!*

Mac: *Good! Now, start the CD player on your computer, turn off the lights…*

CelticRose: *I've already done all that, Mac. Hee hee*

Mac: *Wonderful! You're anxious tonight, my sweet!*

CelticRose: *Mac, I've waited for this all day.*

Mac: *Read my words, Rose, and feel my touch as I begin by kissing your lips. Do you want me? Do you need me?*

CelticRose: *Oh Mac, I need you more than life itself!*

He smirked when he read those words. She just didn't know how prophetic her words actually were.

When CelticRose had typed out her final moans, Mac was nearly ready to type in yet another private message box. Now he could devote his attention to SexyLove.

[205]

God, these screen names are really stupid! Can't they come up with something with a little more pizzazz? Like mine. It's funny that none of the women ask what MAC stands for. They probably think that's my real name. This has gotten almost too easy. No challenge! Oh well, what do I expect from bored, lonely housewives with low IQs?

Well, let me get rid of Rosie so I can move on.

Mac: *Rose?*

CelticRose: *Yes, darling?*

Mac: *Have I made you happy, my love? Are you satisfied?*

CelticRose: *Yessss! I'm floating! You make me feel so desirable, so wanted. I just wish I could meet you in real life.*

Mac: *You don't know how I've wished the same! Is it possible? Can I actually see you, gaze into your lovely eyes, touch your silky skin?*

CelticRose: *Oh Mac, I'm so afraid I'll disappoint you. I'm not beautiful like you think. It's only your words that make me feel that way.*

Mac: *Oh no, Rose, I'm certain you are as lovely as I imagine, but physical beauty is only a package we use to house our souls. I want the woman inside, the one I've loved for so long. I want to hold you, tell you how I truly feel. I've hesitated to say this, afraid I'll frighten you...*

CelticRose: *Mac? What is it? Please tell me!*

Mac: *Rose, I think I love you.*

CelticRose: *Ooooooh Mac, I KNOW I love you! And yes, I want to meet you, to hell with the rest of the world. I'm dying to be with you.*

Mac: *My love, your words make my heart sing! Is it true that we are really going to be together? Please assure me you are serious!*

CelticRose: *Yes Mac, I mean it. Where and when?*

Yes, it was becoming too easy.

~

After arranging a time and place for their meeting, Mac *kissed* her goodnight, changed his nickname so CelticRose would think he was no longer online, then opened the private message to SexyLove.

No, no challenge. Perhaps one day he would meet a woman worthy enough to be his opponent in this game. Until then he would have to content himself with lesser players.

~

CelticRose not only showed up at the hotel, she was almost thirty minutes early. Mac chuckled to think she was in such a hurry to reach eternity.

He opened the door and wasn't even surprised to find an overweight woman wearing stirrup pants and an oversized T-shirt. She smiled nervously, clutching the straps of her straw purse in her pudgy hands. She looked at him, registered the fact that he was tall, handsome, and very sexy. He knew she suddenly felt very fat, and very ugly. She nearly stepped back, poised to run back to her car in the parking lot.

As if he sensed this, Mac reached out, took her hand, and brought it slowly to his lips, all the while gazing into her eyes.

"Rose! Come in, my lovely lady. I've been so nervous, waiting for your arrival."

Her laugh was shrill and she was nearly shaking her head in denial that this gorgeous man could still say that after seeing what she looked like. No man had looked at her like that in many years, and it made her lonely heart swell with gratitude and desire.

"I'm sorry. I told you I'd disappoint you…"

He pulled her into the room, closed and locked the door behind her, then wrapped his arms around her abundant waist.

"Do I look disappointed, love?"

"Well no, but…"

"No, I'm pleased, my beauty! I've waited so long for this. Now, no more words. Just let me kiss you. I want you so badly…"

"But Mac, don't you want to know my real name? I want to know yours…"

Nibbling on her neck, which elicited moans from deep in her throat, he whispered, "You are now, and forever will be, my CelticRose. I need no more than that, and I can't ask for more."

He led her to the bed, gently lowering her large body to the cool, crisp sheets. As he stood in front of her, he began to slowly remove his clothing while whispering words of love that resounded in her love-starved heart.

She reached down to pull the T-shirt over her head, but he placed his hands over hers. "No, my lovely, allow me to do that. As I said, I've waited a long time for this and want it to proceed just as I dreamed it would."

She giggled as he pulled the shirt up, then grunted as she had to rise from the pillow to allow him to slip it off. Still wearing her black stirrup pants and her bra, she was surprised when he settled his weight onto her prone body. She had expected him to completely remove her clothing before he got this far.

Before she could question him, Mac began to kiss her with passionate intensity, his hands caressing her neck, his thumbs stroking her jaw-line.

"CelticRose, I've imagined how wonderful this was going to be and you've lived up to my expectations. It is exactly how I knew it would be."

"Please Mac, tell me your name. Or at least tell me if Mac stands for something else."

The thumbs increased their pressure, the strength of his touch beginning to frighten her. She pushed her head into the pillow, trying, in vain, to escape the squeezing fingers on her neck.

"Mac? What are you doing?"

He straddled her body which now had begun to thrash upon the bed, pinning her to the mattress. His fingers tightened and he delighted in the blue tinge that began to rapidly infuse her face.

"Mac! Ugggg...Ma..."

"So, CelticRose, you want to know what MAC stands for, huh? Okay, *darling*, I'll tell you. It stands for Macabre. Do you even know what that means? Oh, how silly of me! Of course you do…NOW."

Her body relaxed in death, just as his did in release.

After he showered, he slipped on his jacket. He took a last glance at the body on the bed.

Looking at her lips parted in death, he chuckled. "Perhaps you should change your nickname to BlueRose."

Still laughing, he got into his car to head home.

Yeah, too easy.

~

Mac had scarcely hung his gun and holster on the wall hook before he was signed on, ready to "chat". It had been a month since CelticRose, during which he had also "met" SexyLove. When he went back into the "chat rooms" where he had met the women, little was mentioned about their absence.

In the open forums, he was the epitome of kindness, intelligence, and compassion. It was there that he had lured the women into the private message boxes.

Mac thought that tonight he would just stay in the open area, not bothering with trying to find a new game partner. He wasn't in the mood to be disappointed again.

As he was typing yet another witty reply to something that had been said, he heard the *ding* that signified an incoming private message.

Frowning, he was surprised when he didn't recognize the nickname at the top of the message box.

SirenSong: **Hello darling**

Mac quickly scrolled the section of names that currently occupied the chat room he was in, but didn't see that particular nickname there.

Mac: **Hello! Have we met?**

SirenSong: **Not yet**

Mac: **Oh? Intriguing! I've never seen your nickname before**

SirenSong: **Oh, but I've seen yours**

Mac: **You have?**

SirenSong: **Oh yes. I've been in several of the chat rooms you were in, but had another nickname at that time. I changed it to SirenSong, hoping to spice up my image. What do you think?**

Mac: *Well, it has certainly gotten my attention!*

SirenSong: *Wonderful-then it works!*

Mac: *Well, I'm happy to meet you, SirenSong*

SirenSong: *And I you, too, love.*

Mac's interest was piqued. Never before had a woman, if this *was* a woman, sent him such a fascinating message.

Ah, I have a new player on the field. Let the games begin!

Mac: *Tell me, SirenSong, what do you look like?*

SirenSong: *<smiling> No, no! Not on our first 'date', Mac! Just allow me to get to know you before we advance to that stage.*

Mac: *You mean you're not curious about what I look like? <grin>*

SirenSong: *Oh, I believe I can imagine what you look like. Want to know how I see you?*

Mac: *Sure baby, tell me what you see in that pretty head of yours.*

SirenSong: *Don't be condescending, Mac. You neither know me or what I look like, so just cut the crap, okay?*

Mac's laugh was the first genuine one he'd had in years.

Oh, a girl with spirit! This may turn out to be the one. Yes, I do believe this is going to be fun.

Mac: *Sorry, SirenSong. You're right. I had no license to say that and I'm truly sorry if I've offended you. Now, since you've obviously 'seen' me online for a while, tell me what you see.*

SirenSong: *That did somewhat pacify me, but do NOT let it happen again, Mac. I won't be talked down to or insulted. Understood?*

Mac: *Yes, understood. Now, what do you see?*

SirenSong: *I see a man in his mid to late thirties, rather tall, around six feet two. You're slender, yet have broad shoulders, with an athletic build. You have brown hair and brown eyes. You think you're superior intellectually to most people, especially to women. You find most of us shallow and frivolous. How close am I, Mac?*

Mac was amazed at the accuracy of her description of him and wasn't quite sure he liked it one bit. But, she had the nerve to tell it as she saw it, something he could appreciate. Here may be a worthy adversary.

Mac: *SirenSong, I'm impressed. You're very close to the mark on most of that.*

SirenSong: *No Mac, I think I'm right on the money. What's the matter? Afraid to admit it?*

Mac: *Sweetheart, I'm not afraid of anything!*

SirenSong: *Ah, which brings me to one other point. I believe you're in a position of authority, such as a security guard maybe.*

~

SirenSong leaned away from the computer keyboard and covered her mouth to stifle the giggles threatening to erupt. Just from bits of information she had gleaned over the last few months, she was fairly sure he was a police officer, so what she had just said would make him irate.

Mac had to squeeze his hands into fists to keep from crushing the keyboard in his rage.

A security guard?   Just who the hell does she think she is?

SirenSong: *Still here, Mac?*

Mac: *Yeah, I'm still here. No, I'm not a security guard. But what does my line of work have to do with any of this?*

SirenSong: *Nothing, really. You just asked me what I thought and I told you. Why so upset?*

Mac: *Not upset. I have to go for now. Lots of stuff to do and several other ppl I need to speak to.*

SirenSong: *Okay. Goodnight, sexy Mac. Talk to ya soon! *Kiss**

~

Mac didn't bother to acknowledge the ending of the conversation or the kiss she sent his way. He was angry but since he was sure he'd want to talk to her again, he felt it best to not alienate her.

Several people were issued citations the next day for things Mac would normally have ignored. He was still irritated with SirenSong. When he stopped to think about it, it seemed silly to get upset with typewritten words on a computer monitor, but he then remembered those were real people on the other end of his keyboard. It was for sure that CelticRose and SexyLove had been real when he killed them.

Mac didn't rush to his PC the second he hung up his holster that afternoon. He knew it was because SirenSong had somehow figured out he was a police officer.

While online, he sought to remain one of the masses, just another assemblage of disembodied words on a screen.

Somehow, SirenSong had seen through that and had reached the core of his being. Mac didn't like that.

He didn't sign on until just before his usual bedtime. He thought that even if SirenSong was online, he wouldn't have to talk to her long since it was so late. He was afraid he wouldn't have the fortitude to break free of another conversation with the lady unless he was summoned away by sleepiness. Within seconds he heard the alert.

DING

SirenSong: *Hello darling*

Mac: *Hi*

SirenSong: *Just "hi"? Is it only me or did the temperature just drop in here? ;)*

Mac: *Sorry, just have a lot on my mind.*

SirenSong: *Have a lot on your mind? It always amazes me that ppl get online when they're preoccupied or have problems. Why not just deal with reality when you're 'off-line? This is the place to play! Come on, Mac, play with me! <EG>*

Mac: *SirenSong, I'm not really interested in 'playing' tonight*

SirenSong: *For some reason, I find that very hard to believe, darlin'*

Mac: *That only proves you don't know me that well*

SirenSong: *No sweetheart that only proves you're afraid of me*

Mac: *I told you, I'm not afraid of anything!*

SirenSong: *Oh really? Then come play with me. I'll play nicely, I promise. I can be a very good girl when I have an incentive.*

Mac: *And just what might that incentive be?*

SirenSong: *A man that knows how to treat a woman like she deserves to be treated*

Mac was starting to warm up to this line of conversation.

Mac: *How does a man do that? With YOU, I mean?*

SirenSong: *Let me begin to explain this slowly…*

Mac: *Yes, do*

SirenSong: *The man in question would hold me, run his fingers through my long blond hair while kissing me, deeply, passionately…*

Mac: *and then?*

SirenSong: *(laughing huskily) Dear Mac! Why don't you just meet me and I'll show you, in real life? I'll love you so well you'll forget where you live!*

Mac's fingers trembled as if with palsy

Mac: *Where? When? Name the place and time. I'll be there*

SirenSong: *Ready to prove you're not afraid of me, huh? Tomorrow night, eight o'clock, on the west bank of King Lake, near that huge tree that was struck by lightning last year. You know the place?*

Mac: *Yes, I know it. It will be interesting to see if you have the nerve to actually show.*

SirenSong: *Don't worry, love, I have more nerve than you could even imagine. Be there!*

DING

The message box was closed with a finality that made Mac almost wonder if he'd imagined the whole thing. He glanced at the clock above the computer and was shocked to see it was almost midnight.

Man, time flies when you're planning murder!

~

Billowy clouds were drifting across the moon periodically, which made the lake seem almost alive with movement. The air was just crisp enough to make a person feel vibrantly alive.

As Mac raised his head, he noticed a movement in the dense stand of trees.

She stepped from the forest into his living dream. She wore a long, white, diaphanous dress, the folds swaying in the soft breeze. Through the gauzy material, Mac could see a strong suggestion of luscious curves that any woman would have died for.

Her loose blond hair reached her waist and her green eyes were large, luminous. When she smiled, it was as if the gods had opened Heaven for mere mortals to glimpse the Promise Land.

"Hello darling."

"SirenSong!"

She seemed to float toward him. He hoped his heart didn't explode.

"Mac, I've waited for such a long time to meet you."

"You have? But you only spoke to me online a couple of days ago."

"Yes, I know but I just waited for the right time."

"The right time for what, lovely lady?"

She walked up to him, pressing her exquisite form to his, and raised her face to kiss him with a sensuousness he'd never felt before.

"For this, my darling."

With those words, she slipped the thin dress from her body, giving him an unencumbered view of a body more lovely than even he could imagine.

"Quickly Mac, remove your clothes!"

"What? Here?"

Her throaty laugh made his pulse race.

"Yes, here. I thought you weren't afraid of anything, darling."

It was the only dare he needed. He stood before her, quaking with a desire he'd never experienced except while ending a life.

When she pressed her lips to his, Mac closed his eyes in bliss. She sighed when she pulled back and he leaned his head back until he nearly lost his balance.

"Lie down, darling. I don't want you to fall."

When he had settled onto the pine needles resting on the forest floor, she lay beside him, caressing him and kissing his throat.

Mac's entire body was rising from the rough ground, moans filling the former still air of the woods.

~

When Mac rose to meet her touch, SirenSong picked up the knife she had hidden in the fragrant pine needles. Just at the moment he was most vulnerable, just as he reached his pinnacle, she drew the sharp blade across his arched throat so that the scent of blood surrounded them.

When she felt the hot gush of blood splash her fevered skin, SirenSong convulsed in that way she could achieve only at times such as this. After the final spasm washed over her trembling body, she walked to the water to bathe.

She then pulled Mac's body to the edge of the water, wrapping a chain around his body that was attached to a concrete block that few would have believed she could have moved by herself.

Watching Mac's body sink, she splashed herself with the cool water to wash away any remaining blood. She remembered to swirl the knife in the cold water to clean it, too.

Back on shore, she pulled the dress back on, a frown marring her face.

Yes, this has gotten too easy. There's no challenge. Maybe someday I'll find a worthy opponent. Men are so easy and can be so stupid.

Dear Boy
by
John Biggs

I'm remembering this: grownups do not like Dear Boy.
They don't like my bent legs that are a little bit too short, or
my arms that are a little bit too long, or my extra thick fingers
that are perfect for dancing an action figure across the table
toward Little Brother's birthday cake.

I kiss the dancing man on his white plastic lips. I tell the
birthday-party-people, "His name is Davy," as clear as the
evening news so they have to listen.

Davy jumps like a ninja spider. He floats like an
astronaut's ghost in orbit around Little Brother's cake. He
pulls my hand behind him the way jet planes pull white lines
across the sky. All the birthday-party-children want to be Dear
Boy—only for a little while, only long enough to fly with
Davy.

The birthday-party-parents want Dear Boy to be
somewhere far away, some place with locked doors and
fences and other boys like me. They read the icing words on
Little Brother's cake; they stare at the two smoldering candles

so they won't have to look at me; they pretend Davy isn't singing, "Happy birthday to you."

He sings louder and the grownups move further away, as far as they can get from the Davy-voice that bubbles in the back of my throat like phlegm.

I try to tell them, "That's how Davy talks," but the words twist around my tongue and come out backwards.

Little Brother laughs. He reaches for Davy and I pull him back in the nick of time. He takes a candle from his birthday cake as if that's what he wanted all along. He crunches it to mush with his Little Brother teeth, as deadly as a shark in the Atlantic Ocean.

Davy tells me, "Little Brother will hate us when he's older, just like everyone else." Davy knows everything I don't.

But Little Brother doesn't hate me yet. He smiles as I crawl onto the table. The grownups pull back a little more in case someone has to stop me.

"Quickly, Dear Boy. Before they organize." Davy's phlegmy voice makes the party people clear their throats.

"Nearly there."

"What's he doing?" someone says from the back row of grownups

"Will he hurt the baby?"

"Why would I hurt Little Brother?" The words come out in grunts and drools.

Before anyone moves my way, I throw my arms around Little Brother and kiss him on the lips. He tastes like candle wax and chocolate icing. Little Brother kisses me back. His kiss is so sweet I forget to breathe.

Davy tells me, "Little Brother steals all the love, Dear Boy. Don't let him take yours."

"Too late," I say with my thinking voice. "He's got most of it already."

"I'm your true and only friend," Davy reminds me. "I'll fix it so you're the best again. Wait and see."

Davy's phlegmy voice worries Mom.

"Get him," she says to everyone and no one.

"Get him, please!"

When she uses the magic word, Da has no choice. He lifts me off the table, holds me away from him, like he does with Kitty when she doesn't want to be picked up. I stretch my neck as far as it will go and kiss Da on the lips. He makes a face but can't pull back—not with the birthday people watching. His mouth tastes like Emily. She used to be Mom's special friend but now she likes Da better. Mom thinks Da will love her again when her *baby fat* is gone.

"Little Brother spoils it for everybody," Davy says.

The Da-kiss goes on and on, even with all the Davy phlegm talk and the sour-milk-taste of Emily. I don't know when to stop a kiss unless Davy tells me, and he's busy telling me bad things about Little Brother.

"Not potty trained, even though he's ready."

"Puts everything in his mouth."

"He's smarter and cuter than Dear Boy and he'll figure that out pretty soon." Davy tells me Little Brothers last forever unless something happens—something no one expects but everyone watches out for."

"Matches, electric chords, choking hazards, stranger dangers." Davy lists them one by one.

When Da finally pulls away. I look around the circle of grownups who can't quit watching me. I search the circle, one face at a time until my eyes find Emily.

I point at her with one of my too-thick fingers and shout, "Whore!" It comes out perfect. Just the way Mom said it to Da this morning.

Every grownup eye is on me now. Hateful eyes. Disgusted eyes. Eyes that want to see me someplace far away.

"An institution," Davy says. "Where Mom and Da will forget Dear Boy forever."

Forever makes the world spin. A sound starts at the back of my throat, like Kitty getting a hairball ready. For a second I think Davy's trying to say something important, then suddenly a protective layer of vomit covers me and Da.

"Saved," Davy says.

Da curses under his breath and carries me to the bathroom to wash away our shame.

~

I'm remembering this: Davy called to me from a toy box in the hospital on the day I met Little Brother.

"Hey there Dear Boy, come and get me."

There were Hot Wheels in the box and Fisher Price telephones and an airplane with a broken propeller, but Davy was the only one who talked.

"Underneath the puzzle game," he told me. "The one with shapes that fit into especially made holes."

I didn't like the triangles and circles game. I didn't want to touch it because sometimes I start playing without meaning to.

"You'll need a true and only friend when they bring Little Brother home," Davy said. "Take me quickly before it's too late."

Da's shadow passed over me like a storm cloud that sends everyone running for the cellar.

"Time to go see Little Brother now." Da was careful not to touch me. Careful not to say my name.

There was Davy underneath the shape game exactly where he said. The whitest white plastic ever. He had a coonskin cap. One hand was at his side and the other was in the air, like he'd been holding something before a bad little boy chewed it off.

I grabbed Davy in the nick of time.

"It's not stealing if the plastic man asks you," I told Da.

The words came out jumbled so he pretended not to hear. He looked at his watch to remind me how seconds turn into minutes. Minutes turn into hours. Hours turn into forever.

"Time to go." He held out one hand so I'd take it. My hand in his, my long arm stretched as far as it would go to make up for my too-short legs. He wouldn't pick me up because that would be like telling everyone I was the best he could do when it came to making sons.

He let me push the buttons when we got to the elevator. I asked Davy if that would change when we brought Little Brother home.

He said, "Everything will change, Dear Boy—everything."

~

I'm remembering this: Kitty has needles in her paws. She chases things across the floor; she pretends they are alive but won't be too much longer.

"Kitty is the best killer ever." Davy shouts from my pocket. Loud, so I can hear him over the television cartoons that Da turns on when it's his turn to watch us. I take Davy out so I can hear him better, which really doesn't change things because his voice comes from the back of my throat.

Kitty likes the phlegmy sound. She stops batting Hot Wheels and bumps her face against mine. She purrs like the refrigerator motor. Warm and friendly, but her breath smells like rotten meat.

Davy says, "Don't let her get me, Dear Boy. She'll chase me under the couch for sure."

That's what Kitty does with everything. There are Hot Wheels under there, and Ben Ten action figures, and marbles from the Chinese checkers game Mom put away after Little Brother learned to crawl. Things have been under the couch since forever, all chased there by Kitty.

Little Brother stops chewing on the leg of a plastic cow and bangs it on roof of his Fisher Price barn.

"Ki . . ." Little Brother reaches a hand in Kitty's direction; he grabs the air with his fingers.

"Ki . . ."

Kitty turns one ear in Little Brother's direction, but the rest of her is pointed at Davy. She nudges him with her paw. She keeps her needle claws safely hidden, because so far it's just a game. When I fly Davy over Kitty's head she stands on her back feet and makes an electric sound, like before she kills a butterfly.

"Ki . . ." Little Brother pushes a button inside his Fisher Price barn and makes a sheep noise that's not as interesting as

Kitty's butterfly killing sound. He throws his plastic cow at me.

"Ki . . ." Little Brother wobbles as he stands. He falls onto his bottom. He stands up again—so interested in Kitty he forgets to cry.

"Dear Boy!" Davy is too nervous to make a plan.

"He wants Kitty, Dear Boy. Stop him!"

What can I do? Little Brother gets everything he wants. My best toys, Da's best smiles.

"Ki . . ." Little Brother wobbles across the room.

Kitty falls over on her side instead of running. She curls her paws, pretending Little Brother doesn't want her. She tries to keep her needle claws from coming out because the worst thing in the world is hearing Little Brother scream.

I try to tell him, "No, no, no," but the no's get tangled up behind my tongue. Finally they break loose at once and come out in a shriek.

"Noooooo!" Not as clear as a television word but it gets Da's attention. It gets Kitty's attention too. Her ears lay back. Her tail twitches like she's getting ready to climb the curtains and doesn't care who's watching.

When Little Brother grabs her, Kitty's needles come out. He screams even louder than I did, but he doesn't let go until she draws scratch lines across his face.

Da moves slow at first, like a train that might not make it to the top of the hill. Then he speeds up, without seeing anything between him and his only perfectly good son.

Da's knee knocks me on my back so hard I drop Davy. Da has Kitty in both hands shaking her, calling her all the "Goddamned" names Mom doesn't like to hear. He opens the sliding glass patio door and tosses Kitty way too hard into a holly bush. He picks up Little Brother, but he doesn't throw him into the holly. He kisses the scratched places. He runs his fingers through little brother's hair. He tells Little Brother, "That bad old kitty lives outside now. She'll never bother you again."

I'm at the patio door, watching Kitty climb out of the holly bush. Davy calls to her but she's afraid to come since Da went crazy.

"Little Brother spoiled things for Kitty," Davy says. She won't come close even when he waves to her with his plastic hand. The reflection of Da's face is big and mean when he looks toward the patio door. Some of the meanness gets through to Kitty but most of it bounces against the glass and falls on me and Davy.

~

I'm remembering this: Little Brother likes plastic action figures. He sits by the patio door watching Kitty through the glass, tapping on it with a green soldier whose head has been chewed off.

Kitty is killing bugs and watching Little Brother in case he's learned to open doors all by himself. He holds the green plastic man where she can see it, twists the soldier between his fingers so his spit reflects spots of sunlight onto the living room ceiling.

"Da's turn to watch us again, Dear Boy." Davy dives off of the coffee table and bounces on the carpet. I pretend it's the Atlantic Ocean full of sharks that will get Davy if he doesn't swim to shore pretty fast. He hops onto my knee in the nick of time, ready for another adventure.

"You never know what is going to happen with Da around." Davy flips into the carpet-ocean again, ignoring the sharks because they are pretend, paying close attention to Da because he's real.

He pays so much attention to Da that he doesn't notice Little Brother crawling across the floor, pretending he's a baby. Babies never get punished for anything, no matter how bad. Dear Boys get punished for everything, even things that aren't their fault. Sometimes Dear Boys get a smack if Mom isn't around to see.

Before Davy can swim to safety, Little Brother has him. Faster than a shark, he puts Davy in his mouth.

"Help me Dear Boy!"

Kitty watches everything through the patio door. Da watches from his Lazy Boy recliner. Kitty can't do anything. Da could help, but he doesn't care if Little Brother chews Davy's head.

I try to shout but the words get stuck. I try to cry, but my tears don't work and Da wouldn't care anyway, so I pretend to be a TV super hero and jump on Little Brother.

Like Super Man. Like the Incredible Hulk. Like the biggest strongest Dear Boy ever. I land on Little Brother and snatch Davy and try to get away before Da knows what's happening.

Not fast enough. Da grabs me by the shoulders and shakes me hard enough to vibrate the world. I make the hairball sound, but my protective layer of super hero vomit won't come fast enough. He pries Davy from my hand and gives him to Little Brother.

"Help me, Dear Boy!"

I don't know what to do and it's hard to think of anything with Da so close and almost angry enough to smack me.

"Help me!" Davy's head is all the way into Little Brother's mouth, but his voice is still in my throat.

Kitty bats at the glass patio door. She has a spider trapped under her paw, struggling to get away, but it's as hopeless for the spider as it is for Davy.

"It's either me or Little Brother," Davy tells me. "Choose quickly, Dear Boy. Who's your true and only friend?"

Kitty bats the spider off the glass. Knocks it under a lawn chair with a killing blow.

Now I know exactly what to do.

I reach underneath the couch, where Kitty has been batting toys forever. Here is a domino. Here is a plastic Ben Ten action figure. Lots of things that Little Brother wants, but there is something under the couch that Little Brother wants even more than dominoes and plastic men. Something I can trade for Davy.

Marbles! From the Chinese checkers game I never learned to play. Put away by Mom because marbles are dangerous.

"Choking hazard," Mom said. Too dangerous for Little Brother to resist. Once marbles get into a little boy's mouth, they go where nothing is supposed to be.

"Save me, Dear Boy!" Davy's head is already twisting on his neck. In another second it will be too late.

"Look!" The word comes out television clear. I roll the marbles against each other on my palm. The click is perfect. The sparkle is even better. Little brother takes Davy out of his mouth, compares the beauty of the marbles to the white plastic face of a half chewed action figure.

The swap goes so fast, Da doesn't know what's happening. In a second, little brother has the marbles in his mouth. In two seconds they are sliding into the danger zone where they will stop him from spoiling one more thing.

He tries to scream but nothing comes out. He tries to cry but he's already blue. Da turns Little Brother upside down, holds him by his legs, smacks him on the back, trying to shake the marbles loose, but nothing comes out.

I hide Davy in my pocket and wait to see what happens next.

~

I'm remembering how grownups love Little Brother best of all. They've dressed him in a special suit and laid him in a shiny wooden box that's only big enough for him. Some of them cry. Some of them touch his face. Some of them tell Mom and Da, "You're still young. You can have more children."

"Dear Boy loves you," I tell Mom to remind her of the son she has who isn't *in a better place.* Dear Boy is here. Dear Boy is now. Dear Boy is forever. I try to kiss her but she cries instead of kissing back. Da takes me on his lap and tells me I'll see Little Brother again someday. He combs my hair with his fingers and sings a song so softly I can't understand the words.

"You won't see him again," Davy tells me. "Never, Never, Never." Davy has a plan.

Everybody hears his voice at the back of my throat and they think I'm crying. They've been waiting for my tears since Little Brother choked.

Mom told Da I couldn't cry because I was in shock.

The doctor told them both, "He doesn't understand. Too young to comprehend, even if he wasn't developmentally disabled."

Now they think I'm crying just like everybody else. Mom kisses me. Da pats me on the back. Strangers gather around and tell me, "Everything will be all right.

Words like *heaven* and *Angel* spin around me like water going down the bathtub drain, and before long I really am crying. Even though I don't want to see Little Brother again, and I don't believe he's in a better place.

"Cry louder, Dear Boy," Davy tells me. I can feel his plastic body pressing on my chest from inside my shirt pocket. I can feel the sharp places on his head left behind by Little Brother's teeth. That makes me cry harder, because those tooth marks are forever and Little Brother isn't.

"Would you like to see him?" Da asks me. "Shall I hold you up?"

I try to say no, but Davy answers for me, a deep and phlegmy, "Hold me up!" as clear as Mom sobbing, "Our baby's dead!"

Da flies me over to Little Brother the way I fly Davy over the pretend Atlantic Ocean, the way I fly him over Kitty's head so she can't bat him under the couch.

"Kiss!" Davy calls out from the back of my throat. He's out of my pocket now, in my hand, moving toward Little Brother like a television super hero flying off to save the day.

"Think it'll be OK?" Da asks Mom. "Think I should let him do it?"

"What harm . . ." Mom's talking like she's not really sure, but she doesn't want to think about it.

"What harm can it do?" she says as Da lowers me over Little Brother. I kiss him on the lips.

Chap Stick, fingernail polish, Black Flag Ant Killer.

"Put me in Little Brother's pocket," Davy tells me. His plan bubbles out of the back of my throat one phlegmy piece at a time.

"You have to do it, Dear Boy."

I want to ask him why, but I'm too full of tears to talk except with Davy's voice.

"Because," Davy answers the question I never asked, "It will break their hearts, Dear Boy. It will make you the best all over again."

[241]

"Forever," Davy says as I slip him into Little Brother's jacket pocket.

"Forever and forever." When they close the box, Davy is inside. It's a better box than the one he lived in at the hospital.

Mom and Da wrap their arms around me, crowd me between them so hard I almost disappear.

"You're the best," Mom says in a bubbly voice almost exactly like Davy's.

"The very best," Da says. All according to the plan.

I'm remembering this: Davy knows everything I don't.

"Dear Boy" was published by Written Backwards in *Chiral Mad 2* on 12/13/13.

http://www.amazon.com/Chiral-Mad-2-Michael-Bailey/dp/1494239973/ref=sr_1_2?s=books&ie=UTF8&qid=1387038288&sr=1-2&keywords=Chiral+Mad+2

"Hiding"

by

Joshua Danker-Dake

She huddled against the cold metal bedframe, shuddering, her face buried in the quilt to muffle her sobs.

Her pulse thudded like blows in her head. Surely he could hear it. She felt dizzy.

His voice thundered through the house. "Where did you go, baby girl?"

She clutched the mattress with tiny hands, pressing into it as though it could possibly shelter her. The bare oak of the guestroom floor was uncomfortably hard under her scraped knees.

"You know I'm going to find you, baby girl! You know that!"

She did know it. There was no escape, only a few fleeting minutes of reprieve. She knew that the longer it took him, the worse she'd pay for it. But she could never bring herself to do anything other than hide.

The floorboards creaked in the hallway, and she clapped her hand over her mouth to restrain a whimper.

Hunkered down behind the bed, she felt rather than heard him look into the room. There was nowhere to go.

But he didn't enter the guestroom. He moved on.

She allowed herself to breathe.

Should she try to move? Under the bed was no good. She'd learned that the hard way when he'd flipped her bed and smashed her lamp. She fingered the scar on her arm as she remembered.

"Baby girl!"

She was unable to stifle her cry when she saw she'd gotten blood on the quilt—the good quilt grandma had made. When he saw that…

"Where are you, baby girl?"

His voice had changed. It was soft, concerned, conspiratorial. This voice made her shiver. It was somehow easier when he was raging.

She touched a finger to her lip and it came away bloody. She hadn't realized...

"You know why we have to do this, baby girl. Let's just get it over and done with."

He was coming back down the hall. His footfalls turned her to ice. He wouldn't miss her a second time.

"You know my heart, baby girl." He was in the doorway again. "You know I love you."

He entered the room, his wide-buckle belt in his hammer fist, and when he saw her, he smiled.

"There you are, baby girl."

Cowering behind the bed, she looked up and up and up at him, a hundred feet high. Her breath caught, and she managed only a single inaudible *please*. Reflexively, she raised a hand over her head in defense against him, as against an avalanche.

He came around the bed. Air found her lungs and she screamed, spewing all her terror at him.

"Daddy, please!"

He swatted her arm away. Impatience broke through on his face and in his voice.

"Come here, baby girl," he said, and took hold of her. "This is for your own good. You know that."

"No, no, no," was her gasping, squeaking litany as he dragged her from the room, but by then, of course, it was too late.

Chosen

by

Marion Grace

A new hole was torn in my soul with the sing-song taunt from my siblings and neighbors, "Hunchback! Always bow. Never chosen anyhow!" They enjoyed pointing out that, as they grew straight and tall, I became more bent over. I hoped to be chosen one day, but that was the fondest hope of everyone. Only the best of the best were chosen. I tried again with all my might to stand tall.

My stunning and ever present mother helped my self-esteem plummet. "A slight storm in life and you're first to hit the ground and the last back up. Your poor posture drags our proud family name through the mud. Stand tall! No offspring of Anemone Coronaria will be a ground gazer."

I wilted.

"Aunt Rose says you are seeking attention and that I should restrict fluids," Mother continued. "She's prickly, but being a social climber, she knows how to be one of the chosen."

I tried again to straighten up. I saw mother smile. Had she noticed me?

"I'm sure your sister Iris will be chosen."

Crestfallen, I held my tongue.

"I'm aware she's a pistil, but she certainly has turgor." Mother's smile vanished as she redirected her attention to me.

"You must improve. You can miss your opportunity and wind up like old Granny Lace." Pointing in her direction, Mother grimaced and shuddered. "Vigilance and preparation are our family's virtues."

I knew that tone. She was building to make an exit. She gracefully turned her face skyward. Once on that trajectory, she would never cast a downward glance at me.

~

The sun-bathed countryside was quiet enough to hear the gentle wind answering the crickets. Here and there, birds called to their own and responded with fitful beginnings of flight. The warm, bright beams of light fell on my face as they filtered down to my secluded level. I drank deeply the moisture-filled breeze as it tickled every inch of me.

I was soaking it all in when my older brother's strikingly full and vibrant face engulfed my field of vision. Sweet

William had a way of being everywhere at once. A many-faceted personality, he often overshadowed me.

"Give up and admit it. We can't all be chosen. You can only work with what you've got." With a slight sway, he bore on. "Lay low while the rest of us find our place in the sun." His friends beckoned and he drifted in their direction.

I found gumption and shouted, "No! I won't curl up and die because you want to spread out. I can put down roots, too." My courage sapped as a new round of "Hunchback" seeped into my hearing. Dew-shaped tears formed on my face. It only led to more scorn.

"That will be quite enough of that!" The commotion reached Granny Lace, even in her bed. Angered, she rose to her formidable stature. "Outward beauty is tarnished by inner ugliness. Only the truly beautiful are chosen." Her flashing gaze silenced everyone.

I loved and respected Granny Lace. She had known many who were chosen. The others had moved away from us, so I whispered a long held question. "Granny, you are lovely inside and out. Why were you never chosen?"

Granny's face softened as she looked at me squarely. "In my youth, I had the same question. I let the wind carry me away with my own self-importance. When I finally put down roots, I found myself between a rock and a hard place. I was a late bloomer and past my prime. I set myself apart, so I was not noticed as others were chosen." There was a glisten of tears in her eyes. Perking up a bit, she said, "My joy is to encourage all of you to bloom where you are planted. We must all strive to be chosen someday. It's our highest calling."

~

Vibrations. Tremors in the ground got stronger. We youngsters were silent with fear, but the more experienced strained upward for a better look.

An elder shouted, "It's coming! Everyone, attention. Only the best will be chosen. Look alive!"

Thuds heralded the approach of something. We were stock-still. A contained darkness grew quickly across the familiar field of my birthplace. It was much smaller than the shade of a cloud.

I gasped. The shadow was from a huge being! Two large appendages allowed locomotion. Two others swooped out of the sky, aimed for everyone I knew in this world. I trembled as the head of the creature lowered toward us. It had a round face, the likes of which I had never seen. I was terrified until I saw the upper appendages caress many of the faces around me. It hummed softly.

"Hello, you lovely ones. Who wants to go into my basket?" It put the basket on the grass near us and continued to compliment each of us. "Oh, you are enchanting. You too. How vibrant you are."

As it picked some from our midst, each one would respond joyfully, "Chosen!" Their voices were a melody. They were all so happy.

Granny's smile faltered as the being drew near her. "Enjoy your success, my dears," she called. I ached for her as I realized this was the meaning of being passed over. She was about to be left behind... again.

The shadow hovered over her. Its voice said, "Well, aren't you precious? What are you doing over here all by yourself?" As it descended carefully around Granny, whose mouth was agape, eyes wide, and arms uplifted with gathering joy, it cradled her and said, "You can come too."

Granny's voice was loud and strong, "Chosen! Chosen!"

Very happy for her, I fought back tears. "Goodbye, Granny!" I resolved to give her a smiling sendoff.

Many were gathered into the basket and congratulations filled the air.

Unexpectedly, the being slowed, turned back, and looked over the rest of us again. "I'm looking for a special one." This time, its descent came farther than before. Everyone around me perked up. It looked at ground level.

What could it be hunting for? I watched with rapt attention.

"There you are! Oh, you're perfect. I'm so glad I found you." Everyone craned to see who had been deemed perfect.

Then it happened. The gentle touch of this creature around my entire self put me in shock. I sang out, "Chosen!" as I was picked and gathered with the rest of the fortunate ones. My smiling face was met with indignant stares and the familiar cold shoulders.

"Perfect, huh?" Iris was stiff with her nose in the air. "You wait until it stops to look at us all. You were picked by a mistake, obviously." She moved away from me.

"You'll get tossed out, you'll see." More than a couple chimed in.

Granny eased her way to me. "Don't you pay them any mind. Being chosen is a great honor. They're jealous because it seemed to want you more." Her scowl silenced them. She turned to me and said, "No one really understands why some are chosen and others are not. In my long life, there have been some surprises as to who was chosen. It's unquestionable that our lives have a greater purpose and it seems to be connected to beings such as this. We will see, soon enough."

~

It didn't make sense that the tops of the trees seemed to be passing by us. Granny saw my puzzled look and smiled. I did feel comforted. "Do you know where we're going, Granny?" At that, everyone's attention shifted to her.

"I can only tell you the legends I've believed all my life. It's a different place from anything we've known. We are part of a magnificent creation. Each of us is unique with value beyond our comprehension. We will get the chance to share that unique gift and then experience a new happiness and fulfillment we can only attain if we have been chosen." Granny hugged me.

Sweet William puffed up his chest and said, "Each of us gives our family name the honor it deserves." Smiles beamed all around. I tried to join with a little smile. After all, I did get picked.

"All except for you, Hunchback."

My smile disappeared, my gaze lowered. I waited for the familiar rant from my brother.

"I can't see why you were included." He folded his arms and glowered.

Granny interrupted his game. "On the surface, you may be exceptional, but you don't want to be narcissistic." Everyone cringed at the thought of *that* name. "Prepare yourselves for whatever comes next. Remember that ugliness in the heart will shine through your face, and that *will* get you tossed out." Everyone was pensive from her warning.

Suddenly the sky was gone! Wood and stone replaced it. The tall creature's face reappeared. It smiled and hummed again. We were picked up together, then placed side by side on a flat surface. One by one, we were selected and placed in a globe of water. In the end, I was the only one left.

I was terrified. Could they have been right? Was I picked by mistake? Would I really be tossed out? Despondency encircled me like a fog. Was I created to be rejected? It was all a cruel joke.

The tall creature called out, "Where are you my little love?"

It picked me up gently. I closed my eyes, ready to be thrown out. Instead, I was put with all the rest in the refreshing globe of water. My placement was on the edge, so that I bent over the side.

The creature gave another call, "I have something to show you."

Granny encouraged me to drink the clear, life-giving water. As I did, I was refreshed, but I was still myself. Hunchback. I tried to raise myself up with everyone else, but I could not.

The creature's face came close to those who stood straight and tall. It inhaled deeply. "Ahhhh." A wide, approving smile covered the large face and the eyes turned up at the corners. It hummed again and moved out of our sight.

Everyone spoke at once.

"We have accomplished our goal!" Sweet William's voice was unmistakable.

"We are the object of joy by just being here." Iris stood in the center of the globe.

"We have made this creature happy." I heard several elated voices say.

I knew my fragrance was not inhaled. Hidden as much as ever in this globe, I made no difference. I was bent over, forever to look at the ground. I was a failure.

As the creature came back in view, it was leading a smaller creature with curly hair, playful eyes, and a beautiful smile. It giggled as it bounced toward us. Tiny fingers gripped the flat surface that held the globe. It stretched up to catch a glimpse of us.

The older voice said, "I picked these flowers out of God's wildflower garden. Aren't they lovely, honey?"

The small creature said, "Purr-ty"

"Yes," the larger being answered. "Now, look at this perfect, special flower." The large hand turned the glass globe so I was in front, looking down at the young one. "I found this flower especially for you, my precious, little Jesus. It's the only one out of all these flowers who could look back at you."

I looked into the face of the little one. I was captivated by the openness and wonderment I saw. He found joy in me! He reached up with delicate fingers and touched my face. Granny Lace was right. I had found my happiness and fulfillment.

Family Treasure
by
Renee La Viness

"The key to the treasure chest is in my Bible."

That was the last thing Grandmama said before she closed her eyes, this morning.

At the end of the day, after the police, the coroner, the funeral home, the phone calls, the intimidating rush of events, Molly sat at the kitchen table, alone in the dark.

I don't want to go upstairs. I'll have to pass her room to get to mine. I just can't. She's not there to tuck in. Molly buried her face in her hands as the tears overtook her.

The funeral home director had said the crying spells would come and go for a few days. Then she would probably experience . . . what was next? Anger?

Blindly, she made her way to the sofa, picked up the remote, and turned on the TV. After realizing she had no idea what day it was, what time it was, or what was on any channel she'd just scanned, she turned the noise off, set the remote down, and sat quietly in the still, dark room.

The dim glow from the nightlight at the bottom of the stairs shone on Grandmama's blue, upholstered rocking chair.

The tears returned. Molly let the grief pass through her body in waves. She was only twenty-five and had no family left. She was all alone in the world.

When the tears subsided, Molly stared at the rocker, where Grandmama had spent her last moments. She'd looked so peaceful, like she'd fallen asleep.

Oh, yeah. The key. Maybe tomorrow. Molly reached for a tissue to blow her nose.

~

The sun's gentle morning rays penetrated Molly's eyelids. She blinked her puffy eyes as she slowly remembered why she stayed on the sofa, then sat up.

The afghan Molly usually wrapped around Grandmama on cold mornings was tucked neatly around Molly, as if someone had covered her while she slept. She looked for signs that someone else was there. The door was still locked and everything seemed unchanged.

She folded the afghan and placed it on Grandmama's chair before shuffling into the kitchen for coffee and toast. It would be strange to make breakfast for only one person.

Somehow, the thought caused her to feel more alone. She wished her friend Izzy wasn't out of town. She really needed an ear, or maybe a shoulder.

Whap-thunk!

The newspaper landed on the front porch and slid into the aluminum storm door. She smiled and waited for Grandmama to say it. And waited.

Then she remembered. How many times would things like that happen before she got used to Grandmama's absence?

"Right on time, as usual." She had to say it. Grandmama had announced it every day since she first moved in. Silent mornings would be hard to accept.

"The key to the treasure chest is in my Bible."

Molly looked up. "Grandmama?" she said, as she rushed into the living room. For a moment, she expected to see the old woman seated in her rocker, waiting on Molly to bring in the paper.

Kneeling by the rocker, she ran her hand along the arm of the chair. The fabric was worn from years of use, but Grandmama had never complained. She loved her rocker. Grandpapa had given it to her for their last anniversary.

"I must be hearing things," Molly said. She brought the newspaper in and dropped it on the coffee table.

"I'm going to get that key out of your Bible, Grandmama," she said to the chair as she headed up the stairs.

At Grandmama's bedroom door, Molly stopped and took a couple of breaths before going in.

She sat on the side of the bed and lifted the worn Bible from the night stand. The pages separated easily, as if they were turned often.

As she flipped through the pages, a book of stamps, an envelope, a picture of her parents, and one of Grandpapa fell out, but no key. She went through it a second time and still no key. The third time, she flipped the pages from the opposite direction.

Molly frowned. Grandmama wouldn't be careless enough to lose a key from her Bible. Maybe she hadn't felt well yesterday morning and didn't notice it had fallen out.

She set the Bible on the nightstand and searched for the key. She looked on the floor, along the bed frame, under the nightstand, and even under the bedspread, but there was no key. After waiting her whole life to look inside the treasure chest, she was going to have to call a locksmith to get inside.

How could Grandmama be so careless?

She reached for the items, to put them back in the Bible. When she picked up the envelope, she saw her name on the front. It was sealed.

Carefully, she peeled it open and pulled out a letter. It was Grandmama's scribbly handwriting.

Dear Molly,

In all your life, I've told you only one lie: There was never a key to the treasure chest. We claimed it was locked because we knew you would believe us and stay out of it. But it is time for you to learn the contents.

When you open the treasure chest, you will find a letter from your father on top. Please read it before viewing anything else.

You have been such a joy to raise and love. We could not have been more blessed as a family.

All my love,

Grandmama

Part of Molly was excited to finally explore the surprises that had teased her mind for so many years. The other part of her was afraid. What had her family kept secret from her for so long? Was it something good? Something bad? She'd waste no time wondering. If she hesitated, she might not ever allow herself to see the contents.

With shaking hands, she placed the letter back in the envelope and made her way to the attic.

Before opening the door, she closed her eyes, said a quick prayer, and turned the knob. There it was, across the room, against the wall.

The box was approximately two feet long and tall and about a foot from front to back. The outside was painted gold with rickrack and jewels attractively arranged on all sides. What child wouldn't want to explore the contents of such a beautiful chest? And to think . . . all these years, it had been unlocked.

She made her way across the room and knelt beside the chest. After kissing the envelope she'd brought with her, she laid it aside. Slowly, she lifted the arched lid.

As Grandmama had promised, an envelope rested on top of the contents. Below it, a large, upside-down box lid was covered with tissue wrapping paper and what looked like hundreds of real gold dollars, silver dollars, and silver half-dollars piled inside. True to the history of treasure chests, this one was filled with real treasure. The sight took her breath away. Maybe it was because her family had collected so many. She stared in wonder, then remembered the letter.

She lifted the envelope and removed the letter inside. Even though Dad had died only a year ago, she felt like she was holding something written many years before. She unfolded the stiff pages and read out loud.

My dearest Molly,

If you are reading this, your mother and I are no longer alive. I hope your life is as wonderful as we've always wanted it to be.

All these years, we have kept a secret from you. Please try to understand our feelings and decisions as you read on. We would never do anything to hurt you. Choices had to be made and we did what we felt was best. Maybe we were right; maybe we were wrong. But we had to make decisions and these are the ones we agreed to. And now, it's time for you to know the truth.

A long time ago, Gloria Wallace, the next door neighbor, was going to have a baby. She was just eighteen, and even though she was about to marry Chester, neither of them had planned on having children. So, they decided to give the baby up for adoption.

Your mother had just been through a hysterectomy and was depressed that she would never be able to have any children.

Molly stopped reading and chuckled. "Silly Dad. You meant to say 'any more' children. She had the hysterectomy after I was born." She smiled at her father's mistake and read on.

We never told you when she had the hysterectomy. You always assumed it was after your birth, but it was actually a few months before.

Molly paused. She scrunched her eyebrows together and cocked her head as if it would help her interpret the words.

You have to understand. Your mother's heart was breaking. It was a time when people didn't talk about medical

operations, so nobody else knew she'd had the hysterectomy. I
would have done anything to take that pain from her.

Molly didn't know whether to cry for her mother's
hidden pain, or hold her breath for what was still to come, but
she couldn't stop reading. She had to know the rest.

Chester confided in me about the baby. It was great
timing. So, they married and we arranged the adoption. We
paid Gloria's medical expenses, and your mother made her
some of the most beautiful maternity clothing that hid the
pregnancy as long as possible. Gloria moved in with her sister
on a farm in another state for the last three months of the
pregnancy. After the baby was born, we took a "vacation"
and came home with our daughter who was born while we
were away. Nobody else ever knew, except Grandmama,
Grandpapa, and the lawyer.

Chester and Gloria started a savings account for you.
You'll find the information in this chest. They also babysat
whenever we needed it. They have been wonderful. And yes,
they are your biological parents.

Inside this treasure chest is your past and an opportunity for an exciting new future. We can't be there for you now, but Chester and Gloria can. They have promised to wait on you to come to them, so they will know it's what you truly want. They love you every bit as much as we do. Your mother and I hope you'll allow them to be part of your life.

Please don't be angry with us. You put living color in our world. We have loved you so much.

God bless you, my baby girl.

Always and forever,

Dad

Molly's hands fell to her lap, letting go of the letter as she looked blindly toward the attic window. Her whole life was a lie. A lie.

"Mom and Dad are not really Mom and Dad. Chester and Gloria are my real parents." Speaking the reality didn't seem to make it easier to digest. "Am I supposed to be happy? Angry? Sad? Grandmama just died. The guy at the funeral home didn't tell me there would be other family losses to affect my emotions. What am I supposed to be feeling? I'm having a major identity crisis, here."

Molly ran to her bedroom and flung herself onto her bed, planted her face in the soft, pink bedspread and screamed loud and long, until no energy or voice remained. Then, she cried for what seemed like hours until she fell into a deep, exhausted asleep.

~

At 5:47 the next morning, Molly finally opened her eyes. Silence roared inside her head and her stomach was competing for *Thunderstorm of the Year*. She hadn't eaten anything yesterday. It was a very emotional day.

She didn't want to get up. Her face and throat were tight, swollen. She drug herself to the bathroom, to see how bad they looked. When she reached the hall, her cell phone rang. She stumbled down the stairs to answer it.

"Molly? Molly, is that you?" Izzy asked. "Are you okay? I called you all day yesterday and you never answered. I knew something had to be wrong."

"I'm okay, Izzy. I'm so sorry. I had a really tough day, yesterday," Molly said.

"I bet you did. And I was out of town. Mom and Dad told me the news when I got home, last night. Are you okay? I'm so sorry to hear about your grandmama. Should I come over?

Wait. Don't answer that. I'll be right there." Izzy hung up before Molly could answer.

~

When Izzy showed up, Molly had two cups of hot coffee and an almost empty box of tissues at the kitchen table.

"You should have called me," Izzy told her. "I'd have come back to town for you."

"I know. But I was lost in the surreal emotions and then—oh, I didn't tell you, yet." Molly gulped.

"Tell me what? What didn't you tell me, Molly?" Izzy set her cup down and looked into her friend's eyes.

"Follow me to the attic and I'll show you."

The girls made their way to the attic and Izzy read the letter. "Is this for real?"

"Dad wouldn't' have written it, if it wasn't."

"Wow. Wow. Just . . . Wow."

"I know."

Silence filled the room and lingered while the girls stared at each other. Neither knew how to break the silence. Finally, Molly spoke.

"Will you stay here with me while I go through the rest of the treasure chest?"

"Of course. I'll stay here until you get sick of me. You'll have to tell me when it's time to go, okay?" Izzy hugged Molly.

"Deal."

After pulling away, Molly took a deep breath and reached into the treasure chest to pull out the box lid of coins. It was reinforced with wood and very heavy. "You'll have to help me count these, later."

"I don't think I've ever seen so many in all my life," Izzy said.

The girls laughed. Molly was relaxing for the first time since Grandmama died.

After going through a couple of envelopes with information about the savings account and other items, they found two jewelry boxes. One was from Gloria and one was from her adopted mother. They both contained jewelry her mothers had purchased for Molly, as well as jewelry from all her grandmothers. Everything was labeled.

Underneath a hand-sewn quilt was another envelope with Molly's name on the front of it. She didn't recognize the writing, at first. "It's from Gloria."

"Do you want me to read it to you?" Izzy asked, reaching for the letter.

"No. Give me a minute. I'll do it. I need to hear her side of the story."

Gloria and Chester had both enclosed a letter. They asked Molly to forgive them for not being the parents she deserved and said they couldn't have found better parents than the ones who had raised her. They hoped she would accept them as her biological parents when the time came for her to know the truth. The quilt was made by both mothers as a gift of love, to represent their agreement to share and love Molly together.

"Are you mad about it? The adoption, I mean?" Izzy asked.

"I don't know." Molly sighed. "I'm trying to be reasonable, but it's hard. My parents lied to me. All of them." She closed her eyelids, but huge tears snuck out the corners and rolled down her face.

"Yeah, but they tried to make it right with all this. And your biological parents stayed close, in case you needed them. And like their letter said, when you had that appendicitis attack and wound up needing blood, Gloria gave her blood for you. That shows she loved you. She didn't have to do that.

And your mom and dad could have made them go away to live." Izzy sat up, tilted her head, and shrugged her shoulders. "I mean, hey, this isn't the most common adoption arrangement, you know?"

"That's true," Molly said. "Why do you always have to make so much sense?"

"I don't normally. You're the sensible one, remember? But you're a bit off your rocker, right now. Somebody has to put you back in place." The girls laughed as they repacked the treasure chest and headed back downstairs.

"I'm so glad you came. I really needed your carefree smile and laughter."

"About your grandmama," Izzy began, as she looked toward the empty rocker. "When is her funeral?"

Molly's stomach sank. "Tomorrow at noon," she said. "It's in the paper this morning. The phone should start ringing any time now . . . as soon as everyone wakes up and reads the news."

As if she'd chanted magic words, her cell phone rang. The girls laughed.

"I'll call them back," Molly said.

Back at the kitchen table, the girls visited between phone calls. After a couple of hours, Molly sent Izzy home.

"Are you sure?" Izzy asked.

"Positive. I'll be okay. I have to get ready for the funeral, tomorrow."

"What about Mr. and Mrs. Wallace?" Izzy asked. "Are you still mad about the adoption?"

"I'll talk to them before the funeral." She hugged Izzy, then accompanied her down the front steps. "I promise I'll be okay. Don't worry."

~

That evening, after dinner, Molly walked next door and rang the doorbell. Gloria opened the door.

Molly cleared her throat and spoke. "I need my family to go with me to Grandmama's funeral, tomorrow."

Author Bios

John T. Biggs is a cross genre writer with 60 short stories published in magazines and anthologies. He's had some luck in contests, including: Grand Prize—80th annual Writers Digest Competition, 3rd prize—Lorian Hemingway Short Story Contest, and OWFI Crème de la Crème Award. John has published two novels, Owl Dreams and Popsicle Styx (Okla Book Award Finalist), and one short story collection, Sacred Alarm Clock. http://amzn.to/1MheUgc

Award-winning mystery writer **Mary Coley** is the author of Cobwebs, Ant Dens, Beehives and The Ravine. She has been a member of Tulsa Nightwriters for 12 years, and is also a member of the Oklahoma Writer's Federation, and Sisters in Crime. Married, with five adult children, she lives in Tulsa. http://amzn.to/1Xu2CTD

Robert Cooper has numerous writing credits, which include dozens of technical and instruction manuals for numerous fortune 500 companies, a published novel called "*Never Let the Meat Touch the Metal*" and a published article in the Tulsa Night Writer's Anthology. He has also written another unpublished novel and a screenplay. He lives with his lady, Janet, in Tulsa, Oklahoma. Robert's link on Amazon. http://amzn.to/1PN4Bjx.

Joshua Danker-Dake is the award-winning author of the acclaimed comic novel *The Retail*. A writer and editor by trade, he also serves as the Strategy and Tactics Editor for *Diplomacy World*, the flagship publication of the Diplomacy hobby. Other things he gets rather excited about include He-Man and the Masters of the Universe, bombastic European power metal, and St. Louis Cardinals baseball. Visit him on the web at www.joshuadankerdake.com.

Marion Grace joined Tulsa Nightwriters in 2014. She is a newly published author with, "Chosen," inspired as an encouragement to her son after a bullying moment. She has a Christmas story, "Oversight," about two bungling angels following their assignments. A murder mystery, "An Act of Kindness" is about a group of retirement home plucky, elderly women who are unlikely heroes. Her dystopia story, *Heartbreak,* has a moral. As the two sexes separate, disaster follows. Marion celebrates forty years of marriage and four gifts from God with her husband in Tulsa, Oklahoma.

Award winning author and humorist **Nikki Hanna** offers presentations and workshops on aging, leadership, women's issues, memoir writing, and why you write. Her works are rich with strong messages and laced with humor. She has a BS degree in Business Education/Journalism and an MBA from The University of Tulsa. Hanna's books *Out of Iowa—Into Oklahoma* and *Red Heels and Smokin'* are delightful memoirs. *Leadership Savvy,*

Capture Life, and *Hey, Kids, Watch This* are packed with insight and novel perspectives on living and aging. (Available on Amazon and Kindle and through www.nikkihanna.com)

Donna Welch Jones is the author of the Sheriff Lexie Wolfe novels. Her fiction has won awards in the Oklahoma Writer's Federation Inc. contest and the *Writer's Digest* National Writing Competition. Donna has been a Nightwriter for ten years and is also a member of Mystery Writers of America. She lives with her husband, Mark, in Tahlequah, Oklahoma. http://amzn.to/1WaNlK0.

A former teacher, **J. A. Kimmel** joined the Nightwriters in 2012. At that time, she had only one writing award, for a national curriculum-writing contest, and three song publications under her belt. Thanks to the encouragement and support of the Nightwriters, J. A. has now had several short stories accepted for publication. She has also earned a variety of writing awards, including a first-place win for children's fiction. Currently, she is writing a children's series, which she hopes to have published in the near future. J. A. serves as editor of *NightScripts* for the club.

Michael Koch has been a member of the Tulsa Nightwriters for five years. He's penned two nonfiction books and stories published in High Hill Press, Static Movement, Full Moon Books, Southeast Missouri State University Press, and Wicked East Press. Mike's also a member of the

Ozark Writers League, Ozark Creative Writers, and the Oklahoma Writers' Federation, Inc. He lives in Coweta, Oklahoma.

Jim Laughter is the author of 10 novels and 1 children's book. A multi-genre published author, six of his novels have reached kindle best-seller status. A Tulsa Nightwriter since 2007, he served for two years as editor of *NightScripts,* the club's newsletter, and as the 2015-2016 club president. Jim retired in 1991 as a Master Sergeant from the US Air Force after a distinguished 20-year active duty career. He lives in Tulsa, Oklahoma with his wife Wilma. Please visit Jim's website, www.jimlaughter.com to read about his books and his life.

Renee La Viness never wanted to grow up, so she stopped at four feet, eleven inches tall. But what is a grownup, anyway? Height? Age? Wisdom? The ability to reach the gas pedal? An award-winning author who has been published in magazines, newspapers, and anthologies, she also enjoys being an editor, contest sponsor/judge, product designer, and instructor who offers helpful writing workshops in her home town. In her down time, she absolutely loves being a granny. Find Renee' online at reneelaviness.com

Barbara Lockett began writing twelve years ago, embarking on her first novel, The Hidden City, published in May 2014. Other novels are in process. Barbara read books about adventures in faraway places including all the adult books written by Kipling and Robert Louis Stephenson. They filled the bookcases in her parents' home. She absorbed the contents from about ages eleven to fifteen. Stephenson wrote some mysteries for which she never found an equal. Here is a link to her novel. http://amzn.to/1ONMNW8.

Dixie Maxwell is a native Oklahoman with plenty of in-laws and outlaws to keep her life interesting. When she isn't walking on the wild side at her acreage outside Tulsa, she writes suspense novels with a bit of romance, and fictional blog stories loosely based on fact. She and her husband like to explore and photograph exotic locations such as Yellowstone, Eureka Springs and Tybee Island.

Rae Neal's first book, Midnight Melodies: *From the Seas and Rivers of Life* was published in October, 2014, and contains international award winning poetry. An ordained minister, she pastored churches in Spain; launched and taught in Victory Bible Institute, St. Petersburg, Russia; worked as a missionary in Costa Rica, Slovakia, Guatemala, England and other countries. Rae, a member of Tulsa Nightwriters for one year, lives with her husband, Terry, in Tulsa, Oklahoma, where she pastors and continues to write free-verse poetry of nature's beauty and the joys, tragedies and challenges which impact our lives.

Joyce Ross has been an active member of the Tulsa Nightwriters and Oklahoma Writers Federation, Inc.

for several years. During her years as a copywriter in Missouri, she often published poems and articles in the real estate magazine where she worked. *A Lesson Learned,* is her first published short story. A love of mystery and romance keeps her writing into the night, while handling insurance claims keep her busy during the day. Joyce lives in Broken Arrow, Oklahoma, along with her husband, Charlie, dogs Beau and Ginny, and tuxedo cats Neo and Canoe.

Carol Lavelle Snow is a former college English instructor who has an MFA in drama. She is a long-time member of Tulsa Nightwriters who has published fiction as well as poetry. Her poetry has appeared in several journals, including *The Lyric, Harp-Strings Poetry Journal,* and *StepAway Magazine.* She lives in Tulsa with her husband Howard and two cocker friends Smart E. Pants and Que T. Pie. http://amzn.to/1N8tXrt

Carolyn Steele enjoyed a career in journalism and commercial art before retiring to pursue a love of writing and genealogy. She has short stories published in sixteen anthologies and has won a number of awards, which includes nomination for a Pushcart Prize. Her writings reflect a childhood steeped in Civil War history and Indian lore. Carolyn presents a variety of programs designed to inspire others to commit family stories to paper and authored the book, Preserving Family Legends for Future Generations, a 2010 First Place winner for

Heartland New Day Bookfest. Visit her website: www.mcarolynsteele.com

Carla Stewart: In a starred review of *Chasing Lilacs*, Publisher's Weekly said, "Stewart writes about powerful and basic emotions with a restraint that suggests depth and authenticity." This debut novel went on to being OWFI's 2011 trophy winner for Best Book of Fiction. Her passion for times gone by is evident in her six novels, several of which are award winning. Carla and her husband live in Tulsa. They enjoy their seven grandchildren, weekend getaways, and searching for that next great cup of coffee. Learn more about Carla and her books at www.carlastewart.com

Beverly Strader joined the Tulsa Nightwriters in 2005. She has written poetry and short stories since childhood, "self-publishing" a book at age four by giving it to the local librarian. Beverly works in the aviation simulation industry and is a long time Mid-Town Tulsa resident.

Gloria Teague is a multiple award-winning author in both fiction and nonfiction, in books, magazines, newspapers and e-zines. She was awarded Tulsa Nightwriter of the year for both 2009 and 2012. She has nine books and over 60 short stories and several articles published. She's a contributing author to Francine Silverman's Book Marketing from A to Z and Shades of Tulsa, an anthology. She had a full page feature article in Woman's World in 2009. For more information about this author, you can visit her website at www.gloriateague.com

Maggie Villines is owner, publisher and editor of a political blog with 9,000 articles in print online. She also authors a blog on books, writing, wine, spirits and food. She has contributed to various local publications writing about wine, spirits and crime. She was the Wine Manager for Oklahoma's largest retail store, Sales Manager of an Oklahoma brokerage, and owner of a fine wine and spirits wholesale operation. An avid reader of both fiction and non-fiction, Maggie is turning a long-time goal to write fiction, into a reality. Her short story, Agnese, in Tulsa Nightwriters anthology, *A River of Stories*, is her first published fiction. She is a native Tulsan.

Though new to publishing, **Michelle Walker** is far from being new to writing. As a child, Michelle loved writing to pen pals, and had as many as 50 simultaneously. She also remembers as a wee little one, sitting on her grandmother's lap while she read poetry to her. When Michelle was old enough, she began writing poetry, many with deep conviction and heart-felt emotion. She hopes you will enjoy the poem she selected for this publication, created in a small apartment on Christmas Day, her first Christmas alone due to a snow storm, desperately missing the sweet hugs of her grandmother.

Award winning author, **Pamela Wetterman**'s twenty-five year career in Customer Care ignited her passion to expose women's' issues of poverty, physical and emotional abuse, and addiction.

Her first novel, *The Artist's Paradise*, focuses on hope for a struggling marriage and emotional abuse. Her second novel explores the threats of a stalker. Look for *Whispers in The Wind* in 2016. Pamela is a member of Oklahoma Federation of Writers and Tulsa Nightwriters for seven years. She lives with her husband, Bill, in Broken Arrow, Oklahoma. Her work can be found on Amazon.at
http://amzn.to/204BmgE

Bill Wetterman is an award winning author, teacher, and speaker. He has been recognized by *Chicken Soup for the Soul, Writers' Digest, and The Oklahoma Writers' Federation* for his writing. Bill has been a Tulsa Nightwriter for seven years and lives with his wife, Pam, in Broken Arrow, Oklahoma. His work can be found on Amazon at
http://amzn.to/1kCJvbQ.